FROM DRIFT TO DISCIPLINE

By Rahul Gupte

FanatiXx® Publication

FanatiXx® Publication

Rourkela | Mumbai | Delhi NCR | Ahmedabad

From Drift To Discipline
By Rahul Gupte

ISBN: 978-93-7406-077-3 (Paperback)
ISBN: 978-93-7406-007-0 (E-Book)

First Edition – 2026

For permissions, inquiries, or feedback:
Email: outreach@fanatixx.info
Instagram: @fanatixxpublication

ACKNOWLEDGEMENTS

This book was written in silence, but it was never written in solitude.

It started when I recognized life for its challenges, interruptions, and unanswered questions. Without that recognition, this book could not have existed. There would have been no moment when I would have stopped and reflected. It is after this recognition that I began this journey that I felt was worth sharing.

I am immensely grateful to my family for their presence, patience, and support that created the invisible structure of this work. Your understanding in times of silence, reflection, and inward focus made this journey possible.

I am grateful to the many teachers, writers, and thinkers of the world. Both known and unknown. Their words, ideas, and wisdom contributed to my understanding over the years. Many of you may never be aware of the role you played. But your influence lives quietly in these pages.

To my friends, colleagues, and well-wishers. For your encouragement, conversations, and trust. Every thoughtful exchange made contributions in ways that you don't realize.

Finally, I accept the practices themselves. Prayer, gratitude, breath, movement, thinking, and reading, these quiet friends eased me in moments when life felt scattered in my heart and reminded me of what was important when clarity was far away.

If this book speaks to you, it is because these practices speak a universal language, a language of patience, presence, and return.
Thank you for being on this journey.

- **Rahul Gupte**

About Author

Rahul Gupte is a Leadership Coach having a corporate experience of more than 27 years in various leadership roles in leading MNCs and Indian companies. He is a lifelong learner and reflective practitioner who is convinced that real change occurs away from the limelight. He believes that real transformation comes in awareness, consistency, and respect for self.

He had been living a great life for years. He was busy and successful. But down the line, he realized that he was letting life pass by. He was just living. Remaining unconscious of how his days were really going. So, he began studying simple daily practices. His goal was simply to bring more clarity, calm, and direction to his days. But this personal experiment led to a slow transformation. His health and performance improved. On both mental and physical levels. And it happened without force, extremes, or restrictive systems.

His work is all about incorporating spirituality and practicality into one's daily life. He focuses on redefining discipline as an act of self-love instead of control. With that focus, he has found a way to live life sustainably, remaining in a constant alignment with self and steadiness. It involves simple practices. Prayer. Gratitude.

Awareness of the breath. Movement. Journaling. Reading. Setting intentional goals for each day.

From Drift to Discipline is his first book. It is a quiet, truthful reflection of a journey lived rather than a guide from the side. Rahul writes for the people who seem to be outwardly smiling, but inwardly restless. People who seek a gentle way of leading a conscious life lived with practice.

INTRODUCTION

The Change That Occurred Quietly

Most transformation books seem to emerge from struggle. There is a crisis. There is a breakdown. And then there is a dramatic turning point. This book did not come from any of it.

There was not a single moment when it all came crashing down. No moment when I had to pick up my life and start all over again. There was no overnight waking up or overnight transformation. Instead, this book was born 'silently.'

It came gradually. It took shape little by little. In tiny understandings. In the soft discomforts of realization. In the moments of questioning internally. It did not come to chaos. It came from an increasing awareness. I could see that everything was fine. But that was on the surface. When I looked deeper, I could understand that there was something in my life that needed attending to.

For a long time, I lived a complete life from the outside. I was busy, involved, productive, and responsible. I fit in, played my roles, and kept myself busy. Yet, despite that outward motion, there was the feeling of internal disconnection. I was doing a lot, and not necessarily living with intention.

My days were full but not fulfilling.

Like many people, I thought discipline was restrictive. I viewed it as something rigid, demanding, and inappropriate to a life already filled with responsibilities. Spirituality, on the other hand, was something distant. For monks, philosophers, or people with far fewer worldly commitments.

And I didn't reject these ideas outright. I simply postponed them.

"I'll get to this later," I told myself.

“Once things settle down.”

"Once life becomes less demanding."

But life seldom lies down and goes to sleep of its own accord.

What I didn't know at that time was that waiting for the perfect time was a kind of drifting. Days were flowing by. Routines were taking shape. Habits were settling in. And it was all happening without choice. I was living a reactive life. I was simply reacting to situations. But I was not planning my days.

The shift happened when I stopped searching for a big solution and began to pay attention to little practices. I didn't try to change all of my life at once. I didn't pursue dramatic systems for productivity and extreme routines. Instead, I introduced simple habits, quietly, gradually, and imperfectly.

I started to pray. Not as a ritualistic prayer. But a time of grounding.
I began being grateful. Not because I had to. But because I had to retrain my mind.
I practiced breathing. Not to master it. But to calm myself.
I walked every day. Not to reach fitness objectives. But to reconnect with my body and thoughts.
I started journaling. Not to write beautifully. But to think clearly.
I set daily goals. Not so that I would put pressure on myself. But to bring direction.
I read. Not with the intent of impressing. But with the aim of growing steadily.

None of these habits were extraordinary in its own right. But viewed together, if practiced over and over, they started to trigger a profound shift.

My health was improved, not radically overnight, but gradually.
My mind felt more peaceful, not silent, but clearer.
My performance got better, not by power, but by concentration.

The most surprising of these was this. The change didn't feel hard. It came quite naturally, once I stopped fighting against structure, when I started to see discipline as care, not control.

This book is not about becoming someone different.

It is about being able to come back to yourself through simple practices that you can repeat over and over.

I am not writing as an expert, an authority. I am writing this as one who walked this path slowly and stumbled frequently, and learned deeply. Everything you will read here is coming from lived experience, not theory.

If you are feeling overwhelmed, restless, distracted, quietly dissatisfied, without even knowing exactly why, this book is for you. Not to spell out how to live your life, but to share what happens when you choose to live consciously.

This is a tale of gradual transformation.

One story of small habits with a big impact.

A story of going from drift to discipline, one day at a time.

Contents

1

The Life I Was Living Unconsciously

For too long, it was like I was living without truly living. Like simply letting life pass by.

The worst part still was that I was not even aware of it at the time. In fact, had someone asked me if I was living well, I would probably have said yes.

I was active, responsible, and reasonably successful by most external standards. I appeared where I was expected to. I fulfilled my duties. I stayed occupied.

And yet, there was something that was missing inside me.

My life was going on, but I was not in it.

Each day began similarly. I'd wake up and immediately feel the weight of the day I'd have ahead. Things to deal with. People to write back to. Problems I'd need to solve. Before my feet hit the ground, my mind was racing. There was no respite between the sleep and the action. No time to settle in for the day.

I didn't enter my day. I was pulled into it.

Mornings passed quickly. What came with them was urgency. Intention always seemed to be missing. I responded to messages, schedules, and expectations. And I did that without ever pausing to ask myself what I wanted to feel. I gave attention to everything without ever questioning if that thing was really worth my attention. The day passed, and I followed.

Evening hours came before I knew it. Often, I felt tired without any real knowledge as to why. Each day used to be extremely busy. But whenever I thought about what really mattered, I felt blank. Very little came to mind. I went to bed hoping the next day would be different. But the problem was I was not doing anything differently.

This cycle played out again and again as a silent one.

At the time in my life, I thought this was normal. I assumed that adulthood was this way. That this was what the rest of my life would look like. Constantly occupied. Mildly stressed. Perpetually distracted. Everyone around me was apparently doing the same thing. So I didn't question it.

What I did not understand then is harsh but true. Normal does not mean healthy. Busy does not mean meaningful.

Physically, I was functioning. But I was not thriving. My body was something I used. But it also became something I did not listen to. Movement was irregular. Some days I was active. Many days I wasn't. Rest was often sacrificed for productivity. Fatigue became a backdrop condition. Something that was there but was ignored.

There were subtle signals: stiffness, low energy, restlessness. None of them was alarming enough to call for immediate attention. So I postponed care. I told myself that I would work on health later, when things were slower, when the responsibilities decreased, when time was available.

Time, of course, never materialized.

Emotionally, I was more reactive than I realized. Little inconveniences annoyed me. Delays unsettled me. I felt rushed, in too many instances, when there was no real urgency. Stress came after me like a shadow, even on days when nothing went wrong.

It was like I was restless all the time.

I didn't feel very unhappy. But I didn't feel very happy either. It was a strange in-between state. Comfortable enough to continue. Uncomfortable enough to feel that something wasn't right.

Looking back, I know where this restlessness came from. It was caused by not being aligned with myself internally. My actions were based on external demands rather than internal clarity. I responded to life but rarely reflected upon it.

My mind was always busy, but hardly at rest.

I took in information unremittingly. News. Conversations. Opinions. Advice. But I hardly ever processed any of it. I hardly seemed to have the time or capacity to assimilate my learning or experiences. I had thoughts. But they were raw. Unresolved. And that created a clutter in my mind.

I seldom stopped to ask simple questions of myself:

How am I really feeling today?

What matters most right now?

What did I learn from this day?

Without this reflection, my days seemed to lose their distinctiveness. One day was almost like another. Weeks blended into months. Time passed. However, growth was slow and unfocused. This is what I now know as unconscious living.

Not irresponsible living.

Not careless living.

But unexamined living.

The worst part of this phase was how acceptable it was. Nothing was visibly broken. There was no crisis that called for change. Life was "fine."

And that is exactly why it kept going.

Drift does not signal itself through noise. It happens quietly.

You don't suddenly go off track. You slowly stop checking it.

I had routines. But they were accidental. I had habits. But they were not chosen by me. I woke up in the same way. I worked in the same way. I rested in the same way. And in that, I never pondered even once if these patterns were serving me at all.

There was no conscious beginning of my day. No deliberate pause in the midst of it. No reflective close at night.

Spiritually, I was unconnected without knowing it. I did not lack belief, but I lacked practice. There was no time for quiet focus each day, there was no time to connect to something larger than myself.

Life was transactional, one item leading to another, one obligation substituting for the next.

I was managing life; I was not experiencing it.

At times, I felt this emptiness, but dismissed it. I told myself that meaning would come later, after achieving some things, after reaching some things, after crossing some thresholds.

But meaning does not come tagged along with achievement. It comes to light through awareness.

I believed in discipline, and I followed it in many ways. I met deadlines. I honored commitments. I handled responsibilities. But I had a lack of inner discipline, the discipline to care for my inner world as seriously as I cared for the outer demands.

I had discipline for work. But not for stillness.

I had discipline for others. But not for myself.

Without internal discipline, even success is restless.

The lack of anchors in my day meant that I was being moved by life rather than moving through it. I let the outside world determine my inside state.

Good days were seen as good because things went smoothly. Bad days became bad because they didn't go as smoothly.

My peace was conditional.

It took time and honesty to see this clearly. And when I did, I did not feel regret. I felt understanding.

I realized that I was not defective. I was simply untrained.

Untrained in pausing. Untrained in reflection. Untrained in self-regulation. Untrained in purposeful living.

This realization was important as it eliminated self-blame. When something is capable of being trained, one can learn it. And if one can learn it, then it can easily be practiced as well.

That awareness was the real starting point of change.

There was no dramatic event that made me shift. No sudden breakdown that required immediate action. What changed was my willingness to look at my life with honesty, without judgment, without excuses.

I began noticing patterns. I began to take note of the way my days began. I started observing my reaction. I started to realize how little space I made for myself.

And in that, noticing a simple truth became clear.

Nothing in my life was going to change unless I changed the manner in which I showed up to my days.

Not in big ways. But in small, consistent ways.

I didn't need to change my life radically. I had to introduce awareness into it.

This chapter is not written to criticize the life that I lived then. That phase taught me something invaluable: that comfort can conceal stagnation and busyness can conceal drift.

Life I was living unconsciously was not wrong. It was incomplete. Acknowledging that incompleteness, with honesty, with compassion, that was the first quiet step towards a more grounded, disciplined, and meaningful way of living.

Only with this awareness did I have the willingness to change. Not because I was dissatisfied.But because I respected my potential as a human being.

And that is where the journey really began.

2

The Cost of Living Without Anchors

The cost of living without anchors is never obvious most of the time.

It does not come as a loss or obvious failure. It doesn't scream loudly and call for attention to itself. Instead, it manifests itself in quiet ways. In small ways. Over time. Often masked as normal life. For a long time, I thought that as long as I was functioning, I was all right. I was fulfilling my duties. I was keeping busy. I was managing expectations. From the outside, there was nothing to worry about.

But gradually, almost imperceptibly, I began paying a price.

The first cost was mental fatigue.

My mind was constantly active and scarcely ever at rest. Thoughts poured out from an endless stream. Unfinished conversations. Tasks to be done. Mistakes made in the past. Things to worry about. There was no clear demarcation between work and rest, or action and reflection.

Even in the instances where I wasn't doing anything, my mind was busy doing everything.

This constant mental activity caused an underlying exhaustion. My fatigue was such that I felt tired even after sleeping. I had less ability to concentrate intensively. My attention was easily fragmented. I went from thought to thought without settling.

Without anchors, moments that keep the mind grounded, mental energy dissipates. It is like a river without banks. Thinning and losing power.

At the time, I didn't see this as a problem. I assumed this was the way modern life was. Everyone I knew seemed to be busy, distracted, and mentally overloaded. I told myself this was the cost of responsibility.

But normalizing something does not make it healthy.

The second price was emotional instability.

Because my days were not grounded in practices, my emotional state was highly affected by things that happened around me. A smooth day lifted my mood. One that was difficult disturbed me. My sense of calm was dependent on the situation rather than inner calmness.

Small disruptions felt bigger than they should have. Delays frustrated me. Uncertainty made me uneasy. I reacted quickly and reflected slowly, if at all.

I was unaware of how reactive I had become because it seemed justified. After all, life was demanding. People were unreliable. Situations were stressful. My reactions were reasonable within the context.

What I did not see was that without anchors, reaction is the default mode.

Anchors such as prayer, breath awareness, reflection, or movement provide space between stimulus and response. Without that space, the response is reflex.

The price that is paid for reflex living is the emotional wear and tear.

Another expense was a loss of clarity.

When life goes at speed without pauses, priorities tend to become blurred. Everything feels urgent. Everything feels important. And when everything is of the utmost importance, nothing is really important.

I was often busy throughout the day. But I was never sure what I had really accomplished. I was able to finish things. I was able to comply with the demands. I was able to stay occupied. But at the end of the day, there was a sense of vagueness.

I didn't have the clarity to explain what was most important to me.

I couldn't readily say what was worthy of my best energy.

I was unable to say with certainty if my actions were congruent with my deeper values.

Without anchors, the days go by without evaluation. There is movement, but no direction.

This lack of clarity had an effect on my decisions. I chose the convenience over the intention. I said yes too much and reflected too little. I put off important but non-urgent things, especially things relating to health, reflection, and inner growth.

Over the period, this caused a concealed discontent.

Not dramatic unhappiness.

Not visible frustration.

But a quiet feeling of being out of harmony with myself

Another cost was physical neglect.
When there are no anchors in the day, the body gets put secondary too often. Movement is skipped. Breath is shallow. Posture suffers. Rest is compromised.

I didn't abuse my body, but I didn't honor it either.
I used it to play and not to live well.
There were days that I hardly moved consciously. Days when I sat for too long, and I wasn't aware of it. Days that I ignored signs of fatigue and pushed through.

The body is patient but it keeps score.
Over time, the lack of daily movement, the practice of mindful breathing, and rest is reflected in stiffness, low energy, and discomfort. None of these was dramatic enough to cause me alarm. But combined, they had the effect of decreasing my general vitality.

Health, I learned later, is not just about not getting sick. It is about remaining alive, lively in its most positive sense.
Without anchors, the liveliness gradually declines.
Perhaps the greatest cost was the loss of connection to self.

When life is lived reactively, there is not much space to ask deeper questions:

Am I living the life that I value?

Am I becoming who I want to be?

What kind of life am I, in quietness, making through my day-to-day choices?

Without reflection, these questions are not asked. And what isn't asked never gets answered.

I was progressing outwards and floating inwards.

This disconnection did not take the form of emptiness as such. It manifested itself in impatience, restlessness, and an underlying unease. There was always a feeling that something needed to be done. But there was no clear understanding of what that something was.

I was busy, but not anchored.

Active, but not aligned.

Another hidden cost was the loss of presence.

Without grounding practices, I was often here, but my mind was elsewhere. When we were talking, my mind was wandering. In moments of rest, I worried. In moments of work, I rushed.

Life occurred, but I only experienced it partially.

Presence is not a luxury. It is the basis for meaningful living. Without it, even good times are fleeting and shallow.

I did not know how much I was missing until I slowed down later.

Living without anchors also impacted my relationships.

When the mind is cluttered and the emotions are reactive, relationships suffer a silent death. Listening is reduced to a surface level. Patience wears thin. Small misunderstandings get blown out of what they are.
I wasn't unkind. But I wasn't always there 100% either.
Anchors develop inner steadiness. Without them, relationships bear the burden of the unprocessed stress.
There is also a spiritual cost, one that is hard to describe but painfully felt.

Without stillness in life, life becomes transactional. Days turn into lists. Meaning is replaced by motion. Connection to something bigger than self is lost, not because the belief is gone, but because attention is not there.

Spirituality, I realized afterwards, is not all about rituals. It is about remembering what is really important, again and again.
Without the anchors, that remembering fades.
The biggest risk of living without anchors is that it feels like it is ok when it's not.

Because the costs are slow to accumulate.
Mental fatigue accumulates silently.
There is a subtle increase in emotional reactivity.

Physical vitality decreases gradually.

Clarity is lost almost without being noticed.

And when discomfort can be seen, patterns are already ingrained.

This chapter is not intended to cause fear and scare you. It is supposed to generate awareness.

Awareness of the costs that we pay silently when we do not ground our days.

Awareness of how easy it is to become reactive in life.

Awareness of the amount of energy lost when days are not structured with meaning

For me, being aware of these costs was not disheartening; it was freeing.

Because once I could see the costs clearly, I saw something else equally important: If the costs were due to the lack of anchors, then the solution was the introduction of anchors.

Not all at once.

Not perfectly.

But gently, constantly, and intentionally.

That realization did not change my life immediately. But it changed the way I looked at my days.

And when perspective changes, behavior eventually follows.

This consciousness formed the basis for the second part of my journey, the point when I stopped long enough to decide that I was going to live differently.

That pause is where the real transformation started.

3

The Moment I Paused

Transformation did not start because I changed my habits.

It began when I paused.

This pause was not dramatic. There was no external event that made me stop. No crisis, no breakdown, no moment in which immediate action has to be taken. It was quieter than that, almost unheard of by anyone else.

But internally, it was a shift.

For the first time in a long time, I stopped. I took a break from moving constantly. I took an honest look at my life.

All I could see was how my days were filled with movement. Tasks followed tasks. Responsibilities flowed right into one another. Any time there was discomfort, I distracted myself with activity. Any time there was uneasiness, I made myself busy.
Busyness was my excuse.

The pause occurred because I realized that keeping busy was no longer working in avoiding the questions that were quietly coming up. Questions I had put aside for years started calling my name, not clamorously, but persistently.

They were simple questions, but disturbing in their simplicity:
Is this the way I want to live my days?
Am I really here in my life?

What kind of person am I becoming as I make my daily choices?
The questions did not arrive with accusations. They arrived with curiosity.
And curiosity, I found out, is so much more powerful than criticism.

The moment I stopped doing something, I wasn't trying to fix anything. I was not looking for solutions or strategies. I was just able to be a witness, and to look and not judge, not feel defensive.

I started observing my days. About how they were actually going instead of just how I thought they were going.

I paid attention to how quickly I was grabbing my phone in the morning.

I noticed how shallow my breathing was.

I was aware of how little time I spent in silence.

I saw how my emotions change as a result of external events.

Most of all, I recognized how little I looked in on myself.

This break introduced a small but meaningful gap. A gap between living on autopilot and living with awareness. It allowed me to see patterns that were invisible before.

Patterns do not change by us fighting them.

They change when we clearly see them.

There was another thing that I understood during this pause. Probably, one of the biggest things. My struggle was not caused by a lack of willpower. I had always thought that discipline meant force. That I had to push myself more. That I had to be stricter.

But force had never worked for long.

What I did not have was willpower.

What I did not have was a structure to support myself.

This insight was liberating.

I realised that I did not have to become a different person by making any radical changes to my life overnight. I just needed to make more effort to add intentional pauses to my days. I just needed to take the time to reconnect with myself.
The pause taught me something else as well:
I was waiting to be motivated to make a change. But what I really needed was clarity.
Motivation is unreliable.
Clarity is stable.

Once I was able to understand the difference between the way I was living and the way I really wanted to live, small actions began, not forcefully, but naturally.

I took some quiet time. Not formal meditation. Not structured practices. Just honest moments of stillness.
At this time, I understood my life was externally controlled and internally abandoned. I was meeting expectations, but did not nurture alignment.

That realization did not lead me to feel guilty. Instead, it made me feel responsible.
I understood that responsibility is never about blame. It is about taking ownership.

I began to ask myself a different kind of question. Not "What is wrong with me?" But "What does my life need right now?"
The answer was clear: My life needed anchors.
Anchors are not unchanging routines. These are tender points of stability. They provide stability in the midst of movement. They enable us to do things without being swept along by circumstances. Without anchors, people, even strong people, drift.

The silence allowed me to realize that spirituality and practicality were not opposites, but complements. Spirituality provided meaning to my actions. Practical habits made my days structured. One without the other was incomplete.

I did not sit down and come up with some elaborate plan. I did not mention dozens of habits or set ambitious goals. That would have overwhelmed me and reproduced old ways.

Instead, I asked a simpler question. I asked myself what the smallest thing I could do to bring awareness into my life.
That question changed everything.
I realized that transformation starts not with intensity. It begins with sincerity.

I chose to start small. Not because I was not ambitious, but because I understood sustainability.

The pause taught me patience.

For years, I had underestimated the power of small, consistent actions. I thought that real change took a big effort. But a big effort does often lead to burnout. Little work, applied every day, brings integration.

I also knew something that was really important during this pause: Discipline is not a restriction of freedom. It creates it.

The right kind of discipline helps to minimize decision fatigue. It calms the mind. It liberates energy for what really matters.

But discipline has to come from care, not control.

The pause mellowed my connection with myself. I stopped seeing myself as someone who needed fixing. I started seeing myself as someone who needs support.

This change of perspective was very important.

From that space of awareness, I started to experiment, ever so gently, without pressure.

I introduced moments of prayer. Not as something to be done out of obligation. But as something to be done from grounding.

I practiced gratitude. Not because I wanted to be positive. But because I wanted to be present.

I paid attention to my breath. Not to be able to master it. But to calm my nervous system.

I began to walk every day. Not to achieve. But to rhyme.
I wrote. Not to impress. But to understand myself.

I make little goals that I can accomplish each day, not to push but to guide my day.
Every practice started as a question, and not a command: What if I do this today?
The pause was what enabled curiosity to take the place of judgement.
And curiosity sustained change.

Looking back, I see that the pause was the most courageous act of all. In a world that values speed to the max, to pause means strength. It demands willingness to listen, to be uncomfortable, to the truth, to oneself.

Pausing did not make my life immediately better.
But it made my life clearer.
And clarity is the basis for meaningful change.

This chapter is important because many people desire to change their lives, but they don't take the time to see their lives clearly. They pursue solutions without knowledge of the problem. They become habitual without being aware.

But change that's long-lasting begins with seeing.

The instant I stopped, I stopped running from myself. I stopped putting off reflection. I gave up thinking that life would automatically line itself up.

I decided to be conscious in my own becoming.

That choice, that quiet, uncelebrated, deeply personal choice, was the real start of my transformation.

Everything that happened afterwards was the result of this pause.

4

Why I Chose Practices

The idea of change in my mind was very different for a very long time. I thought any change required willpower.

For me, not having a habit or routine translated to being indisciplined. I told myself I must be stronger. I pushed myself to be more determined and consistent. I used to think that everything would fall into place only if I pushed myself.
This belief remained with me for years.

And consequently, for years, it worked quietly against me.

Every attempt at change was the same. I would feel motivated and make a plan, and promise myself a fresh start, and then struggle to stick to it, too. Some days went well. Many didn't. Slowly, enthusiasm died down, and I reverted to old ways.
Each time this happened, I assumed it was me.

What I didn't know at the time was that willpower was never intended to bear the burden of day-to-day living.
Willpower is a finite resource. It fluctuates according to mood, energy, stress, and circumstances. It works best in short bursts and not over long periods of time. Asking for willpower to maintain change is the same thing as expecting inspiration to show up every morning on time.

Eventually, it doesn't.
When I took a step back and reflected upon my previous attempts to change, I noticed something important. The problem wasn't effort. The issue was reliance on force.
Force creates resistance.
Practices create flow.

This realization transformed the way I went about discipline completely.
I started to realize that the most consistent people were not necessarily the strongest or most motivated. They were the ones

who had structured their lives to make it easier for them to make good choices and to repeat those choices.

They did not live by how they felt.

They were depending on what they practiced.

This distinction was of the utmost importance.

Willpower asks the question "Do I feel like doing this today?"

Practice asks, "This is what I do, how can I do it gently today?"

One is conditional.

The other is identity-based.

When I took my focus off willpower and placed it on practices, something softened inside me. The pressure to perform decreased. The fear of failure had loosened its grip.

I was no longer trying to conquer myself.

I was learning to be self-supporting.

Practices, I found, have three powerful properties that willpower has none.

First, practices are repeatable.

A practice does not have to be perfect. It is just that it needs to be returned. Even if performed imperfectly, it reinforces a pattern. Over time, repetition creates familiarity and familiarity creates comfort.

I did not attempt to pray intensely every day. I aimed to show up.

I did not intend to write brilliantly. I aimed to write honestly.
I did not aim to walk far. I aimed to walk daily.
By lowering the bar for success and raising the commitment to consistency, I took the emotional burden that was attached to action.

Second, the practices generate rhythm.
Human beings respond well to rhythmic things. When something becomes part of a daily rhythm, it tends to lose its status as an extra task and becomes part of the natural rhythm of life.
Willpower interferes with rhythm by requiring effort.
Practice creates rhythm with participation being invited.

Once prayer, walking, breathing, and journaling became rhythmic, I didn't spend time debating whether or not to do them. The question went from "Should I do it?" to "When Should I do it today?"
That shift alone saved immense amounts of mental energy.
Third, practices affect identity.
This was the most profound change.

Every time I was practicing, no matter how little, I was casting a vote for who I was becoming. I was no longer someone out for discipline. I was somebody who practised discipline in a gentle way.

Identity does not change through intention, but through repetition. I didn't wake up one day and feel disciplined. I also became disciplined through small acts of care that I practiced every day. Another key insight during this phase was learning the distinction between pressure and structure.

Pressure says, "You have to do this, or you have failed."
Structure says, "This is here to help you."
My previous efforts at change were pressure-driven. Missing out on a day was feeling like failure. Falling off routine was to me like a defeat. That sort of thinking left consistency shaky.
Practices, on the other hand, allowed for flexibility without abandonment. Missing a day was no longer an occasion for quitting. It simply meant returning.

That mindset was liberating.
I also realized that spiritual growth and practical discipline follow the same principle - it is grown through gentle repetition.
Spirituality is not nourished by fits and starts of intensity. It is perpetuated by everyday memory. Practical effectiveness is not developed through sporadic effort. It is constructed by constant habits.

Practices are at the nexus between the spiritual and the practical. They turn an intention into action.

They make awareness embodied.

As I started implementing practices into my life, I saw something unexpected. My resistance reduced.

Earlier, the concept of discipline seemed heavy. Now, it felt grounded. Instead of asking myself to be anyone other than who I was, I was just asking myself to show up as I was.

Practices met me where I was.

I also learned to make the practices small by design.

I resisted the temptation of doing too much too soon. I had learned from experience that ambition without sustainability leads to burnout.

So I chose those practices which were:

Simple

Accessible

Repeatable

Forgiving

I let practices grow organically. Some days had more substance than others. Some days were minimal. All days counted.

This way, I build trust in myself.

Trust is an underrated component of discipline. When you keep small promises to yourself, over and over again, the silent growth of confidence occurs. You start to believe that it's possible to change, not because you're motivated to, but because you have evidence that it's possible.

Over time, these practices started to impact the way I approach anything challenging. Instead of reacting in impulse, I paused. Instead of fighting things to make solutions work, I had a moment of reflection. Instead of putting the blame elsewhere, I changed my inner state.

The external world did not suddenly get easier.

But I became steadier.

That constant changed everything.

Perhaps the biggest thing I learned from the idea of practices over willpower was this: discipline does not have to be harsh.

We often think of discipline and punishment, discipline and control, discipline and denial. But the discipline that changes is compassionate. It understands human limits. It respects energy. It allows rest.

True discipline is not domination.

It is about devotion to your well-being, being clear, and your growth.

Discipline that comes from care is supportive, not suffocating.

As the days became weeks and weeks became months, I saw how these practices changed my life in quiet, unseen ways. They created space where there was no space. Calm where there was chaos. The direction to which there was a drift.

And all of this occurred without heroic effort.

That is the power of practices.

This is a very important chapter because many people fail not because of a lack of desire, but because they rely on will-power alone. Willpower fades. Practices remain.

Practices do not ask "Are you strong today?"

They ask, “Can you return today?”

That question can always be answered.

Choosing practices instead of willpower was one of the kindest decisions that I made for myself. It made it possible to make the change sustainable, humane, and deeply embedded in people's everyday lives.

And once this foundation was in place, everything else, prayer, gratitude, breath, movement, and reflection, found its natural place. From here, the journey is more tangible. Each practice begins to take shape, not as a rule, but as a relationship.

And that is where real change takes place.

5

Prayer - Creating Stillness Before the Day Begins

Prayer was not the first habit that I consciously decided on. It was the one that chose me, slowly, deliberately.

For a long time, prayer existed in my life only on the margins. It came here and there, in hard times, on festive occasions, or times of uncertainty. It was something I turned to when I needed help, reassurance, or strength.

But it was not part of my daily rhythm.

In my head, prayer was a part of another sort of life. One that was slower. Quieter. Perhaps less demanding than my own. I thought I was too busy to do it. I thought that prayer required a certain state of mind. A certain discipline. A certain purity that didn't come all the time to me.

What I did not know at the time was that being prepared for prayer is not necessary. It creates readiness.

At the time I started my journey to living more intentionally, I wasn't seeking out a path of more spirituality. I was just searching for something to start my day in a calm manner. My mornings were hectic, reactive, and mentally cluttered. Before the day had even started, I was on the back foot.

I wanted one thing more than anything else, a still beginning.

That desire took me to prayer, not as a belief system, but as a practice.

At first, prayer was a foreign experience. Awkward, even. Sitting quietly, free from distraction, trying to focus my restless mind. Thoughts raced. Impatience surfaced. Silence felt uncomfortable. But I stayed.

Not because I was disciplined but because I was curious.

I did not come to prayer as a request list or a ritual to be done correctly. I approached it as pausing, a moment to get out of the noise and into awareness.

Prayer is not about saying the right words, I discovered. It is about creating space.

Space before the day begins. Space before decisions are made. Space before the demands of the world enter the head.

That was a space that changed everything.

In these early days, my prayer was simple. Sometimes it was nothing but silence. Sometimes it was gratitude. Sometimes it was a silent recognition that I did not have to do it all alone.

There were times when my prayer was a few minutes long. There were days that it lasted longer. There were days when it was deep, and there were days when it was just mechanical.

All of them counted.

The value of prayer was not how it felt. It was there in the fact that I showed up.

Slowly, prayer became my first anchor for the day.

Before checking my phone. Before getting involved with the world. Before coming on board with responsibilities.

I began with stillness.

That stillness did not take challenges out of my life. It changed how I met them.

Prayer brought about a subtle, but powerful change in the posture of my inner self. Instead of starting the day in the reaction mode, I started it in the receptivity mode. Instead of steeling myself for what was to come, I centered myself in presence.

I stopped asking "What do I need to control today?"

And started asking, "How do I show up today?"

This shift brought about a decrease in anxiety that I did not expect.

Prayer reminded me that I was not the centre of everything, that I was a part of something bigger. That reminder brought humility, and with it, relief. The pressure to manage everything eased.

Spiritually, prayer linked me back to meaning. Practically, it helped me get my focus better.

It created alignment.

One of the most important things I learned throughout this phase was that prayer does not require belief; it requires sincerity. You do not need to subscribe to a particular philosophy or follow a particular format. Prayer is meeting yourself where you are.

Some days, my prayer was structured. Some days it was spontaneous. Some days it was silent.

All of it was prayer.

The discipline of prayer was not to extort devotion. It was about commemorating the start of the day.

I started seeing a difference in my days when there was prayer.

On days that I prayed, I was calmer. I reacted less impulsively. I

listened more deeply. I felt grounded when things went wrong.
On days when I skipped prayer, the difference was there, not dramatic, but real. I felt slightly rushed. Slightly scattered. Slightly disconnected.

This contrast taught me a good lesson: prayer was not an optional decoration. It was a foundation.
Prayer did not add time to my day. It added depth to it.
Another subtle change that prayer brought was clarity. In stillness, priorities emerged naturally. What was really important became more obvious. What didn't matter lost its grip.
Prayer did not provide me with the answers. It gave me perspective.

And often, perspective is more valuable.
I also saw from prayer that I was more tenderly related to myself. I became less brutal, less challenging. I stopped regarding every mistake as a failure and started regarding it as feedback.

Prayer made me compassionate, for myself and for others.
That compassion bled over to my interactions. Conversations became less reactionary. Listening became more patient. The responses became more thought-out.

It was not prayer that made me passive. It made me centered.

One misconception of prayer is that it takes away ambition or dulls drive. My experience was the complete opposite. Prayer made clear to me my ambition. It brought effort into line with purpose.
I still worked hard. I still pursued goals. But I did so with less inner turmoil.

Prayer gave meaning to effort.
Over time, prayer was less about asking and more about remembering. Remembering what was important. Remembering who I was apart from roles and responsibilities. Remembering that life was not just a series of tasks to be completed.
This remembering had a cumulative effect.

Even brief periods of prayer, done daily, produced internal stability. Like a compass, prayer helped me reacquire my bearings again and again.
There were times when prayer was dry. Days my mind wandered off endlessly. Days when silence felt heavy.
I didn't consider those days as failures. I treated them as a part of the practice.

To me, prayer is not about controlling the mind. It is about witnessing it.
The act of sitting, even though there was restlessness, was itself transformative.

Prayer also taught me to be patient. Stillness cannot be rushed. Presence cannot be forced. These qualities develop slowly, through constant practice.

In a world that values speed, praying invites slowness.
That invitation is radical.
As prayer settled down into my life, other habits took on their natural influence. Gratitude became easier. Breathing became deeper. Journaling became more truthful. There was a quieter rhythm to my whole day.
Prayer set the tone.

It whispered, “Begin gently.”
It reminded me, "You are not alone".
It grounded me in, "This moment matters."
This chapter is important as prayer is often misunderstood. It is either viewed as a deep religion or as totally irrelevant. In reality, prayer is all too human.

It is the act of pausing. The act of acknowledging. The act of aligning.

You do not have to know how to pray. You just need to be willing to be still.
Prayer does not require being perfect. It rewards sincerity.

For me, prayer became the doorway - the way in which the rest of my practices came. It was the first step towards leading a conscious life. It transformed the mornings from hurried beginnings to grounded beginnings.

And from that still beginning, the rest of the day went with more clarity, calm, and purpose.

Prayer did not change my life radically. It changed it in silence, one morning at a time.

6

Gratitude – Training the Mind to See Abundance

Gratitude did not come naturally to me.

Not because I was ungrateful by nature. But because my mind had been trained to think like that. What was missing? What was coming? What could go wrong? I was more focused on noticing problems. I hardly ever acknowledged what was already working.

I did not wake up each day thinking negatively. But my own attention was drawn naturally to concerns, pressures, and expectations. There was always something to be fixed. Something to be improved. Something to worry about.

Gratitude, I thought, was a pleasant idea. But it did not seem like a practical one.

It felt passive. Almost naïve. My assumption was that gratitude was something people said when they were successful, not when working. Something that is reserved for times of comfort, not for times of uncertainty.

I was wrong.

When I started living a more conscious life, I am grateful to say that gratitude crept into my life almost accidentally. It was not introduced as a philosophy but as a simple daily practice. And like most simple practices, its power only manifested itself in repetitions.

Initially, the idea of gratitude felt forced.

My mind balked whenever I tried to think of anything that I was grateful for. My mind told me that it was all fake. That I had bigger fish to fry. That no real issues would get resolved if I acknowledge the good and positive things.

But I did press on. Not because of conviction. But because of curiosity.

What if I just practiced gratitude every day, regardless of how I was feeling?

That question changed everything.

I started small. Very small.

Some days, gratitude was acknowledging the fact that I woke up healthy. Some days that meant enjoying a quiet time. Other days, it was as simple as being thankful for the simplest of things. For a meal. A walk. A kind interaction.

I did not look for extraordinary reasons to be grateful.

I focused on the ordinary.

And gradually something shifted.

Gratitude did not take the challenges out of my life. It changed the relationship of my mind to them. Instead of viewing life as a series of problems to be solved, I started viewing it as a balance of effort and support, difficulty and grace.

Gratitude trained my attention.

I saw that the mind goes in places where attention sits. For years, my mind had been focused on 'lack'. Lack of time. Lack of ease. Lack of control. Gratitude was a simple shift. Of attention to the sufficiency.

Not excess.

Not a denial of difficulty.

But sufficiency.

This simple shift deeply impacted how I felt.

My anxiety began to settle as gratitude became a part of my days. Not because problems disappeared. But because my nervous system stopped functioning in constant scarcity-mode.

Scarcity says, "There is never enough."
Gratitude says, "There is enough to start out with."
That difference is subtle. But it is life-changing as well.
One of the biggest things that gratitude has taught me is this. Gratitude is not a reaction to life. It is a way of seeing life.

Gratitude will remain postponed forever when you wait for things to become perfect in life to feel grateful for them. Gratitude is different. It is about feeling grateful for things that are already there, even if they are imperfect.

At first, I practiced gratitude very consciously. I wrote it down. I said it silently. To help me do this, I intentionally reminded myself.

Over time, it became natural.
I saw little things more easily: the heat of the sun, the sound of my breath, the comfort of familiarity, the privilege of choice. These things had always been around. I had simply stopped seeing them.
Gratitude brought me back to my life.
Another surprising benefit of gratitude was how it affected contentment.

Before this practice, my happiness usually depended on progress. I was good when things moved forward and restless when things stalled. Gratitude brought about a shift in my baseline. It made it possible to have contentment with ambition.

I could strive and not feel deprived.
I was able to work without feeling empty.
I was able to wait without becoming frustrated.
Gratitude did not take away my desire to grow.
It eliminated the desperation of growth.
This balance was of the utmost importance.

Practically, when I was grateful, it improved my relationships. When you consciously appreciate the things people bring to your life, interactions soften. Expectations reduce. Conversations get colder.
I became more patient.
More understanding.
More present.
Gratitude also decreased comparison.

When the mind is rehearsed in the awareness of abundance, comparison no longer has a hold. Instead of comparing my life with others, I became more involved with my own journey.
This brought peace.

Another important realization was that gratitude is not about ignoring pain. It is about holding together the pain and appreciation.

There were days when things were heavy. Days of challenges weighing on me. Gratitude did not ask me to deny those feelings. It simply asked me to also be aware of what was still steady.

Even on hard days, something was there supporting me: the breath, my body, a conversation, a quiet moment.
Gratitude made resilience possible.

I also noted how I was feeling physically as a result of gratitude. My breathing became deeper. My body relaxed more easily. Tension reduced.

Perception is responded to by the body. When the mind changes from threat to appreciation, the nervous system follows.
This is where gratitude gets very practical.
It is not just a mindset.
It is a physiological reset.

After some time, gratitude ceased to become an exercise. It began to feel like a lens.

I didn't have to keep reminding myself all the time. My attention naturally went back to appreciation. It happened especially when I realized I was going off track into complaint or frustration.
Gratitude did not eliminate negative thoughts.
It balanced them.

This balance shifted the way I dealt with challenges. Instead of asking, "Why is this happening to me?" I started to ask, 'What's this teaching me?' or 'What do I have left, even now?'
Those questions are rooted.

One of the most powerful effects of gratitude was the way it grounded me in the present moment. Gratitude is not possible in the past and future. It exists only in the 'now'.

By practicing gratitude on a daily basis, I spent more time in the present, and the present is where life actually happens.
Gratitude also helped me to connect spiritually on a deeper level.
It changed the expression of prayer from asking to acknowledging.

From seeking to recognizing. It nurtured humility, not in the sense of being shrinking but in the sense of having a clear vision of life.
I started to find life not something I controlled, but something I was involved in.

This brought ease.

There were times when gratitude was mechanical. Days when I wrote it down emotionless. I did not resist those days. I trusted the process.

And like any practice, gratitude works through consistency, not intensity.

Even mechanical gratitude keeps the door open.

This chapter is important because gratitude is frequently misunderstood to be a personality trait and not considered a trainable skill. In truth, being grateful is a discipline.

What you constantly see shapes your inner world.

Gratitude taught me that abundance is not something that we acquire. It is something that we recognize.

By training my mind to see what was already present, I limited mental noise, emotional strain, and inner resistance. Life became lighter. Not because it got easier. But because I stopped lugging around the weight I didn't need to carry.

Gratitude did not dramatically transform my circumstances.

It changed the way I experienced them.

And that made all the difference.

With the help of prayer, I learned to start my day in stillness.
With gratitude, I learned to build my way through my day with appreciation.

Together, they established a solid foundation of calm and clarity, upon which the next practices could naturally develop.

7

Breathing – The Forgotten Superpower

Breathing was always there. And that was exactly why I ignored it. For a long time, I had been breathing. But I rarely thought about it. It simply happened. In the background of life.

I am breathing, everything is alright. This is what I used to think. I thought, why waste my time thinking about something so automatic?

However, I did not know a profound truth at the time. The way of breathing determines the way of life.

When I began to breathe consciously, I understood what it meant. My breath reflected my inner state. Shallow. Rushed. Irregular. I breathed the way I lived. Quickly. Unconsciously. Never pausing. Stress tightened my chest. Anxiety shortened my breath. Urgency made my breathing erratic. And since I never saw it, the circle was continuously going on.

The body was reacting all the time.
The mind was following.
Initially, I could not make out the connection. I used to think like most other people. Solve problems. Control situations. Complete tasks. It will bring you peace. It would keep you calm.
But that never happened.

Breathing became a part of my life. Not as a wellness trend or something to perform. But something required.
When I started to notice the restlessness within myself, I understood that my body carried nothing that was visibly wrong. All it carried was stress and tension.

Shoulders were tight. Jaw was clenched. Breath was shallow. My body was always ready for something.
That realization was disturbing. I was not consciously anxious. But my body acted as if it were under full-on pressure all the time.

This is the time when I started to pay attention to the breath. Not to change it. But to just notice it.
At first, awareness was strange enough. Sitting quietly and watching my breath caused discomfort. I realized how restless my body was. Thoughts surfaced. Impatience arose. I wanted to do anything, everything but be on my breath.
But I stayed.

And in staying, I found something important.
The breath is always telling the truth.
The mind can rationalize.
The emotions can fluctuate.

But the breath tells the truth of the current inner state.
When the breath is shallow, something inside is locked up.
When the breath is rushed, something inside is hurried.
When the breath is held, there is something inside that is going against it.

This awareness in and of itself was powerful.
I began noticing my breath during the day, not only when it is quiet, but in the middle of activity. Before meetings. In times of tough conversations. While waiting. While walking.
The pattern was clear - whenever stress increased, my breath shortened. Whenever there was an increase in pressure, my

breathing got irregular.

It was the body that was reacting more quickly than the mind.

This is where the breathing went from awareness to practice.

I did not take complicated techniques. I did not tally breaths obsessively or strive for perfection. I simply introduced the conscious breathing - slow, deep, and intentional breaths at regular intervals.

Sometimes it was a couple of breaths in the morning.

Sometimes it was during a break in the middle of the day.

Sometimes it was a moment before responding.

These were short-lived moments, but their impact was cumulative.

Conscious breathing did something remarkable - it interrupted reactivity.

Between stimulus and response, breath created space.

That space changed everything.

I began to realize that many of my reactions were not conscious choices. They were physiological reactions.

Tight breath induced tension. Tension triggered reaction. Reaction shaped outcomes.

By controlling my breath, I controlled my reactions.

This was deeply empowering.

Breathing taught me a lesson that calm is not something you think your way into. It is something that you breathe your way into.
When conscious breathing became a daily practice, I noticed the changes in my body. My nervous system had begun to settle. I was more calm. Not in a dramatic way. But in a steady, grounded way. My inner state remained balanced even in critical and demanding situations.

Conscious breathing did not help me get rid of the stress. But it increased capacity.
Capacity to pause.

Capacity to be intelligent in responding.
Capacity to be present amid pressure.
This capacity had a direct impact on the performance.
I saw that when I was breathing well, I was thinking well. Decisions felt less rushed. I listened more attentively. I spoke more deliberately.

The quality of my presence was enhanced.
Breathing also helped to reconnect me with my body.
Before this practice, my body was something I carried around, something I used as a vehicle for my mind. Through breath awareness, the body was now an ally. I started listening to its signals instead of overriding its signals.

Fatigue became a message, not an obstacle.

Tension became information, not irritation.

This shift created respect for my body and its rhythms.

One of the biggest life lessons that breathing taught me was a lesson on letting go.

Each exhalation is a release.

Each pause is a surrender.

In a life that is so controlled, planned, managed, breath reminded me that not everything needs to be held tightly. Some things need to be let go of over and over again.

Breathing became a daily reminder to soften up.

Breath became a bridge spiritually. It linked stillness and action, prayer and movement, awareness and involvement. Breath was always there, in silence and activity.

It made spirituality practical.

I no more required special conditions of grounding for myself. I carried the tool with me, unnoticed, invisibly.

This accessibility was an important factor.

There were points where feelings were overwhelming: anger, frustration, and anxiety. In the past, I would have immediately reacted. Given conscious breathing, I learned to wait long enough to choose.

Not suppress.

Not deny.

But regulate.

Breathing did not lift emotions.

It gave them the freedom to move and not to overwhelm me.

This changed my relationship with difficult feelings. I stopped fearing them. I trusted that I would be able to breathe through them.

Breathing also improved my physical well-being. My posture improved. My sleep deepened. My energy stabilized. These changes were slow but significant.

The body thrives on oxygen and rhythm. Conscious breathing re-establishes both.

Over time, the breathing became part of my daily flow. I did not schedule it rigidly. I used it naturally, at transitions, before tasks, and after challenges.

It became a part of my way of being.

I learned that breathing is not something that you do occasionally.

It is something you return to.

On days when I neglected to, the difference was obvious. I felt rushed. Scattered. Less patient. Breath reminded me to come back, to the present moment, to my body, to myself.

This chapter is important because breathing is easily underestimated. It is considered too simplistic to make a difference. Yet, it is one of the most powerful levers we have for regulating the inner state.

Belief is not necessary for breathing.
It does not require time.
It does not require tools.
It only requires attention.

Through breathing, I learnt that being calm was a skill. Presence is a practice. Regulation is learnable.
Breathing became my quiet superpower, not because it was dramatic, but because it was always there.

With prayer, I learned to start my day in stillness.
With gratitude, I learned to see abundance.
With breathing, I learnt to be regulated within movement.

Together, these practices built a foundation that was strong enough to support the next step in my journey, getting the body to move consciously.

That is where walking came into my life, not through my exercise, but through my rhythm.

And that is where we go next.

8

Walking – The Discipline That Needs No Equipment

Walking crept into my life unobtrusively.

There was no great intention behind it. I did not start walking with fitness goals, step-counts, or performance in mind. I did not set goals or deadlines. I just started to walk because both my body and my mind needed to move, and walking seemed accessible to me.

That did not require preparation.

It did not require motivation.

It did not ask me to be someone other than who I am.

It only asked me to begin.

Before the practice of walking, movement in my life was inconsistent. Some days I was active, too many days I was not active. Physical activity was based on mood, schedule, and energy levels. If the day was busy or tiring, then movement was the first thing to go away.

I treated movement as optional.

What I did not realize at the time was that movement is not an additional activity; it is a regulator. It controls energy, mood, clarity, and even emotion. When movement is lost, imbalance gradually occurs.

Balance was reintroduced by walking.

At first, it was almost too simple, walking in a way that mattered. I doubted that something so mundane could make a real difference. In a world obsessed with intensity and optimization, walking seemed understated.

But that understated quality proved to be its finest quality.

Walking involved no bargaining with my mind. There was no inner debate on equipment, time slots, or readiness. I could walk anywhere at any rate any day.

Walking removed excuses.

I began with short walks. There were some days that were longer and some that were shorter. I did not judge either. The only intention was to be consistent.

And consistency is where transformation lives.
As walking became an integral part of my day, I noticed that something changed. Not only physically. But mentally and emotionally.

The first to change was mental spaciousness.
Walking created space in my mind that sitting could not. As my body moved, thoughts began to untangle. Ideas surfaced naturally. Problems that felt heavy indoors felt lighter outside.
Walking did not compel clarity.
It invited it.

There was something calming deep down about the sound of steps. One foot after another. No rush. No destination except the walk itself.

The rhythm calmed my nervous system.
I learned that much of my mental restlessness was caused by being physically still for too long. The mind requires movement to process. Walking permitted it.
Emotionally, walking became a release.

The stress that built up silently throughout the day had an outlet. Tension softened. Irritation eased. I did not have to analyze my emotions during the walk. The work was done by the movement itself.

Walking taught me that emotions do not always need understanding.

Sometimes, they require movement.

Physically, the benefits were gradual and unmistakable. My energy stabilized. Stiffness reduced. Sleep improved. I felt more connected with my body.

But perhaps the most profound effect of walking was on discipline.

Walking taught me the nature of sustainable discipline.

Unlike rigid routines requiring strict adherence, walking accepts flexibility. I could walk slowly or quickly. Alone or with company. In silence or reflectively.

Walking is adapted to life and not demanding that life adapt to it.

This flexibility led to humane discipline.

Walking had also changed the way I related to time.

Before walking became a practice, I used to think I did not have time to move. But walking taught me that movement never steals your time. Instead, it creates time. After a walk, I was more focused, more efficient, and more present.

Time expanded by the fact that my mind was clearer.

Walking also helped me to become more aware of the present.

As I walked, I was aware of simple things. The feel of my footsteps. The feel of the ground. The feel of air moving, breath moving. These sensations made me anchored in the now.

Walking became a moving meditation.

I did not have to close my eyes and withdraw from the world. I was all engaged with the environment and with myself.

This engagement brought joy.

Not excitement.

Not thrill.

But a joy that's quiet, steadying, and grounding.

Walking also fits in with practices that I already have.

Prayer grounded my mornings.

I was grateful, and that changed my perception.

My nervous system was regulated by my breathing.

To walk, all of them were united in movement.

In walks, prayer became reflection. Gratitude came without being forced. Breath found its rhythm. Everything integrated.

Walking was where practices met life.

Another important lesson that walking taught me was patience.

Walking does not pressure you to get results. There is no instant reward. Benefits get accumulated slowly, quietly, almost invisibly. This slowness retrained my expectations.

In a culture of instant results, the practice of walking reminded me that some of the most important changes take time, and time invested compounds.

Walking also reconnected me with simplicity.
There was nothing to measure performance. No comparison to make. No outcome to chase. Just movement for the sake of moving.

This simplicity was eminently liberating.
Walking granted me permission to be ordinary, and in my ordinariness, I found balance.

As walking became a part of my daily routine, I noticed the impact it had on my thinking.

Problems did not seem so overwhelming. Decisions were more grounded. It was easier to be creative. The mind functioned better when the body was in motion.
Walking proved the lesson that productivity does not necessarily come from effort.

Sometimes, it comes from flow.

Walking also had an impact on my emotional strength.

On hard days, walking was a refuge. It did not solve problems, but it softened their grip. It reminded me that I could continue, even when things weren't certain.

One step at a time.

This metaphor was not limited to the act of walking. It influenced the way I came at life.

I stopped awaiting immediate clarity.

I gave up on demanding immediate change.

I trusted gradual progress.

Walking taught me how to keep on going without forcing.

With time, walking ceased to be a habit and began to be a friend. It supported me through busy days, reflective moments, and emotional transitioning silence.

I missed it when I didn’t walk. Not out of guilt, but out of awareness.

That awareness was an indication of integration.

This chapter is important because walking is frequently underestimated. It is regarded as too basic to be transformative. But transformation does not necessarily come from intensity. It is often a result of consistency in simplicity.

Walking does not demand discipline.
It cultivates it.
Walking does not exhaust willpower.
It restores it.
Walking does not distract from life.
It reconnects you to it.

Walking helped me learn differently. I understood that discipline can be gentle. I acknowledged that movement can be mindful. And I could see that progress can be quiet.

Walking gave my days rhythm.
It gave my body respect.
It gave my mind space.

And from that space, the next practice emerged naturally, one that required stillness again, but of a different kind.
That practice was journaling, meeting myself on paper.
And that is where we go next.

9

Journaling – Meeting Myself on Paper

Journaling was the one thing that I resisted the most.

Not because I doubted the value of it. But because of what I was afraid I might discover when I slowed down long enough to write. Writing felt exposing. Honest. Unavoidable. When you write, you cannot hide behind busyness or distraction.

The paper does not argue.

It reflects.

For a long time, I thought that journaling was for those who wrote, or thought, or had something profound to say. I told myself that I

wasn't good with words. I assumed journaling required structure, language, and insight, all of which were intimidating.
What I did not understand then was that journaling is not writing well.

It is about seeing clearly.
I did not start journaling because I wanted to create something beautiful. I began because my mind needed a place to unload itself. Thoughts were piling up at a faster rate than I could process. Emotions hung around unresolved. Decisions were heavier than they should have been.
My mind was crowded.

Journaling presented an easy solution: take what is inside and put it somewhere safe, on paper.
At first, it felt awkward. I gazed out at blank pages, at a loss for words. My thoughts were not organized. I worried about whether what I was writing was making sense. Some days, I wrote very little. Other days, I wrote messily.
I allowed all of it.

That permission was of great importance.
There is no need for coherence within journaling.
It creates coherence.

I began with simple entries. Sometimes it was only a few lines about how I felt. At times, it was a description of the day. Sometimes it was a list of concerns, questions, or unfinished thoughts.

There were no rules.

What mattered was honesty.

As I went on in journaling regularly, I began to notice something somewhat subtle but very powerful. Writing slowed my thinking. Thoughts that were overwhelming in my head became manageable on paper. Emotions that felt heavy had lost some of their intensity once expressed.

Journaling provided distance.

Distance is not being detached.

It means perspective.

By having my thoughts written down, I was able to see my thoughts rather than be consumed by them. I could question them. Understand them. Sometimes even laugh at them.

This shift altered my relationship with my inner world.

Before journaling, I had the feeling that my thoughts were absolute. They felt like truths. After journaling, they felt like proposals, ideas to be examined, not commands to be obeyed.

This was a freeing realization.

Journaling also helped me to identify patterns.

Patterns of thinking.

Patterns of reacting.

Patterns of avoidance.

I noticed recurring worries. Familiar fears. Repeated frustrations. Seeing these patterns written down made them visible, and what is visible can be worked with.

Without the journaling, these patterns were quietly occurring in the background. With journaling, they came into awareness.

Awareness is the beginning of change.

Another important benefit of journaling was emotional regulation. There were days when emotions were mixed, stress was mixed with irritation, fatigue with doubt. Writing enabled these feelings to become untied. I did not have to label them correctly. I just needed to get them written out.

Emotion moves when it is acknowledged.

Journaling became a safe place where nothing was supposed to be resolved immediately. I did not need answers. I needed expression.

That alone brought relief.

Over time, journaling became not about unloading but listening.

As I slowed my writing, the insights came through naturally. I started seeing the relationships between how I felt and how I lived. I saw the effect that lack of rest had on my patience. How unspoken expectations caused resentment. How clarity reduced anxiety.

These insights did not come dramatically.
They came up, soundlessly, line by line.
Journaling also helped me to get into a better relationship with the truth.

When thoughts remain in the mind, they remain vague. On paper, they demand clarity. Writing forces honesty. You can't fool on paper, not for long.

This truthfulness was not always comfortable.
There were days when journaling revealed things I didn't want to say. Avoiding fear. Impatience. Inconsistency. But rather than judging myself, I learned how to observe.

Self-compassion was a skill taught to me through journaling.
Compassion is not founded on overlooking flaws.
It is a result of acknowledging them gently.
I stopped using journaling to beat myself up and started using it to understand myself. This change transformed everything.

Practically, journaling was an enhancement in decision-making. When faced with the choices, I wrote about them. I investigated my motivations, my fears, and my expectations. Writing down things slowed down impulsive decisions and brought out what was significant.

Decisions were less reactive and more aligned.
Journaling also complemented my other practices beautifully.
Prayer grounded my mornings.
Gratitude influenced my perception.
Breathing was used to control my nervous system.
Walking cleared my mind.

The practice of journaling brought them all together.
After stillness, gratitude, breath, and movement, journaling became the place where it all came to rest.
It became my daily check-in.

I did not journal for hours. Sometimes it only took ten minutes. Sometimes less. The amount of time was much less important than the consistency.

Consistency built trust.
I was trusting that if something was bothering me, it could wait till journaling time. I had faith that things would be clear, not

immediately, but in time.

This trust amounted to less mental noise throughout the day.
Journaling also helped me to track growth.
Without reflection, progress is invisible. Journaling made progress visible, not leaps but shifts. My tone softened. My concerns evolved. My thinking became clearer.

Looking back at previous entries was humbling and reassuring. I could see how far I had come, even when it didn't seem to be much of a day-to-day.

Growth is seldom dramatic from the inside.
Journaling helps you to recognize it.
One of the most powerful things I've experienced from journaling was how it has helped me to have a better relationship with silence.
Writing is not noise.

It is structured silence.
In a world of constant input, journaling provided me with output.
That balance mattered.
It curbed the desire to be constantly stimulated. It was giving me the ability to sit with myself without discomfort.
Journaling was also a way to further my spiritual awareness.

It became a type of dialogue, not only with me, but with something deeper. Writing after prayer was different. Insights came more naturally. Questions softened.

Journaling came to be a contemplation.
There were days when journaling was mechanical. Days when nothing meaningful came out. I did not resist those days. I trusted the process.

Journaling, like all practices, works through accumulation.
Even blank days count.

This chapter matters because journaling is often misunderstood as an intellectual activity. In truth, it is a relational practice, a relationship with oneself.

It teaches you to listen before reacting.
To reflect before deciding.
To understand before judging.
Journaling does not solve all problems.
It makes them approachable.
By meeting myself on paper each day, I reduced inner confusion and increased clarity. I learned to hold my experiences with patience and curiosity.
Journaling did not change who I was.

It helped me see who I already was.

And that clarity made the next step natural.

Once my thoughts were clearer, my days needed structure, not rigid schedules, but gentle direction. That direction came through setting and reviewing daily goals.

That is where we go next.

10

Daily Goals – Designing the Day Before It Designs You

For a long time, I thought that goals were for the future.
I thought goals were for years, not days. They were things that you would set at the start of a year, just the beginning of a project, or a new phase in your life. Daily life, on the other hand, was too unpredictable to plan meaningfully. I have assumed that the day takes on its own shape for me and I merely react to it.

That assumption defined my life more than I knew.
Most of my days were reactive. I woke up with some vague intentions, but no clear direction. Whatever was felt to be urgent

needed attention. Whatever came loudest got handled first. By the end of the day, I was tired, but often unsure of what I had exactly accomplished.

I had been living in my days, not leading them.
Daily goals crept into my life rather silently, like the other practices. Not as a system of productivity, or even a tool for performance, but as a means of bringing intentionality to day-to-day living.

At first, I resisted the idea.
I was concerned that there would be pressure from setting daily goals. I was afraid that it would make my day a checklist and remove the spontaneity from my day. I thought goals would make me rigid, not free.

What I finally found was just the opposite.
Daily goals did not restrict my day.
They clarified it.

Before, without daily goals my mind was carrying too much. Tasks floated around in no order. Important things compete with trivial things. Everything was equally demanding.
Daily goals gave my mind somewhere to put things.

I started off with a simple question each morning: What truly matters today?
Not what is urgent.
Not what others expect.
But what matters?

This question alone altered the way that I approached my days.
Some days, the answer was work-related. Some days, it was personal. Some days, it was rest, reflection, or presence. I did not try to balance each and every day. I aimed for alignment.
Alignment meant that the day was an expression of my values, even if it was in small ways.

I kept a few daily goals intentionally. Usually three. Sometimes even one.
I was quickly taught that too many goals dilute focus. It is a few, meaningful intentions that create clarity.
Daily goals were not about doing more.
They were about doing what was important.

I also have changed the way I define a goal.
Earlier, goals were a heavy thing, something to be achieved, something to be completed, something to be conquered. With daily goals, I changed them to intentions. They were not demands. They were directions.

This change led to a decrease in resistance.
A goal was no longer a judgment on my worth.
It was a directive for my attention.
That distinction was important.

As I practiced setting daily goals with consistency, I realized there was a subtle change to my mornings. Instead of feeling spread out, I felt oriented. I knew what was worth my energies. I knew what could wait.

This clarity helped to minimize mental noise.
Even on busy days, having clearly-set goals brought back calmness. When unexpected demands emerged, I could decide consciously whether to engage or defer, as opposed to automatically.

Daily goals gave me a choice.
Another important aspect of such practice was the daily review.
At the end of the day I took a few moments to reflect, not to judge, but to observe. I asked simple questions:

What did I do well today?
What moved forward?
What didn't, and why?

This review was gentle. There was no self-criticism. The focus was on learning though, not on evaluation.

Reviewing my day helped me to see patterns. I saw that I was always putting off certain tasks. I could see myself when I overcommitted. I saw when my energy was low.

Such awareness provided for adjustment.

Days pass unconsciously without review.

With review, days evolve.

Daily goals also helped me have a better relationship with time.

Earlier, time felt scarce. There was never enough. With everyday objectives, time seemed organized. I quit filling my day with unrealistic expectations.

I learned to respect limits.

A respect for limits is not a weakness.

It is wisdom.

By setting goals for the day, I was able to cut the frustration. Completion became satisfying. Progress felt tangible.

Small wins accumulated.

Daily goals also helped me build up my discipline, quietly.

Discipline did not feel like forcing myself to do things that I didn't want to do. It felt as honoring commitments that I had made willingly.

This difference changed my experience of effort.
Effort that is in line with intention is light.
Daily goals also provided continuity from day to day.

Instead of beginning each day from scratch, I continued learning. Unfinished tasks were not failures, but information. I made the necessary adjustments the following day.
This continuity led to reduced guilt.
Guilt thrives in vagueness.
Clarity dissolves it.

Another surprising way that daily goals helped was on presence.
When I knew what was really going on, I was able to be completely present to it. I was less distracted. Less mentally scattered. Less likely to multitask for no reason at all.
Presence deepened quality.

Daily goals also provided better decision-making. When opportunities or distractions arose, I was able to ask, "Does this serve today's intention?"
That one question saved an enormous amount of energy.
Not everything needed a yes.

Not everything required immediate attention.
Daily goals allowed me to say no to others and to frivolous

demands placed on myself.

This permission was freeing.

Spiritually, daily goals were teaching me about stewardship of time.

Time ceased to be a feeling of something that happens to me. It was like something given to me. Each day became a space to be lived. Not perfectly. But intentionally.

This changed things with respect to my relationship with responsibility.

Responsibility no longer seemed burdensome.

It felt meaningful.

There were days I wasn't able to accomplish all my goals. I did not consider those days to be failures. I treated them as feedback.

Why did this not happen?

Was the goal unrealistic?

Was my energy misjudged?

Was something more important to emerge?

This inquiry built up self-awareness.

Daily goals also worked beautifully with journaling. Writing goals helped the intention. Reviewing them brought deeper insight. Together, they constituted a loop of awareness and action.

And I also noticed that daily goals had an impact on my emotional state.

When the day was directed, anxiety decreased. When there was a purpose to the effort fatigue was different. Even tiredness was satisfying when it was tiredness from doing good.

Daily goals didn't help me get rid of stress.

They reduced confusion.

And confusion is often more exhausting than effort.

Over time, daily goals became less about productivity and more about integrity, living in alignment with what I valued.

Some days, my most important goal was rest.

Some days, it was a focus.

Some days, it was a connection.

All of these were valid.

Daily goals honored the whole person, not just the performer.

This chapter matters because many people feel overwhelmed, not because they lack time, but because they lack direction. Without intention, days design themselves, and often not in ways that serve us.

Daily goals are a simple way to reclaim authorship of your day.

They do not require ambition.

They require honesty.

They do not demand perfection.

They reward presence.

By designing my days consciously, I began designing my life gradually. Not through grand plans, but through daily alignment.
One day at a time.

Daily goals did not make my life rigid.
They made it clear.
And clarity, as I learned repeatedly, is one of the most underrated forms of freedom.

With daily goals in place, the next practice emerged naturally, the one that nourished the mind and expanded perspective quietly over time. That practice was reading.
And that is where we go next.

11

Reading – Feeding the Mind Daily

Reading had been irregular in my life for more years than I can remember.

I read when I found something interesting. When there was time. When I felt like reading. Books came along sporadically in my life. Enthusiasm at the outset. Neglect soon after. I admired people who read regularly. But I also assumed they had more time, more discipline, or fewer distractions.

I told myself that I would read more someday.

That someday rarely arrived.

What I did not know at this time was that reading is not about time or motivation. It is a matter of priority and intention. Just as physical nourishment requires regular meals, mental nourishment requires regular input.

The mind, like the body, is always being fed, consciously or unconsciously.
If we do not take what feeds it, the world chooses for us.
Before reading was a daily activity, my mind was constantly thinking, but without discernment. News, opinions, messages, conversations, and digital content streamed in a never-ending loop. Much of it was fragmented, reactive, and superficial.

I was informed, but not enriched.
Stimulated, but not nourished.
Reading came into my life as a corrective to this imbalance.
At first, I did not have the intention of reading much. I did not have page goals or reading schedules. I simply made it a commitment to read something every day, even if it was just a few minutes.

This commitment altered my relationship to knowledge.
Reading became less about finishing books and more about the intentional feeding of the mind.
I started making deliberate choices on books on spirituality, psychology, leadership, health, philosophy, and life. I read slowly.

I paused often. I reflected on what I read.
Reading became no longer a consumption.
It became a conversation.

One of the first things that I noticed was how reading changed the way I thought.
Thoughts became more organized. My vocabulary got enhanced , not just in the literary sense, but also in ideas. I came to find words for feelings and experiences that I had felt but never expressed.
Reading gave style to intuition.
It also brought calm.

Unlike digital content, which is a scattergun of attention, reading is a focus. Sitting with a book taught my mind to focus on one thing. This one-pointed attention was profoundly healing.
Reading became a mental standing still.

I noticed on days that I read, my mind was less cluttered. I reacted less impulsively. I thought more clearly. Reading created an inner spaciousness that lingered for a long time after the book was closed.

Reading also increased my self-awareness.
Many times, I came across passages that seemed to have been written for me. Ideas mirrored my struggles. Insights came back to

my questions. Reading reminded me that my experiences were not alone.

Others had followed similar paths.
Similar questions had been asked by others.
Others had struggled, reflected, and grown.
This realization provided comfort.
Reading diminished loneliness, not through offering answers, but companionship.

Another significant change was the way that I was approaching reading itself.
Earlier, I was under pressure to complete books. If I started something, I thought I had to finish it, no matter how relevant or how timely. This created resistance.
Over the years, I let go of that pressure.

I gave myself permission to read slowly.
I allowed myself to reread.
I allowed myself to stop if a book no longer served me.
Reading became responsive rather than rigid.
This flexibility enabled consistency.
I also learned to read with application, rather than accumulation.
Instead of trying to chase down more information, I tried to concentrate on pulling out one idea and live with it. I asked simple

questions.

How does this apply to my life?

What does this invite me to reflect upon?

What little action does this imply?

Reading was transported from intellect to integration.

This approach fit right in with my other practices. Journaling was helpful to me in processing what I read. Daily goals contributed to my application of insights. Gratitude and prayer gave life meaning.

Reading became part of an ecosystem, not a standalone activity.

Another subtle benefit of reading was the impact on humility.

Reading made me reacquire the knowledge that there is so much to learn. It softened rigid opinions. It expanded perspective. It reduced the desire to be right and the willingness to understand.

This openness did improve relations.

I listened more.

I judged less quickly.

I responded in a more thoughtful way.

Reading also built patience.

Books unfold slowly. They reward attention in the long run. In a world of instant gratification, reading taught my mind to place depth over speed.

This patience extended to other areas of life.

I gave up rushing to conclusions.

I gave up demanding immediate results.

I trusted gradual growth.

Reading also affected my spiritual life.

Spiritual reading, in particular, added depth to prayer and reflection. It provided frameworks, metaphors, and language that enriched my inner dialogue. It reminded me that spirituality is not a way out of life; it is a way of engaging with life more fully.

Reading based spirituality on wisdom.

At the same time, effective reading sharpened through practical reading. Leadership insights to make better decisions. Psychological understanding enhanced emotional management. Health-related reading improved self-care.

Reading balanced the inner and outer world.

I also noticed the effect reading had on my emotional tone.

The mind accepts what it is constantly doing with. By giving it something to feed, something to think about, something that was reflective, my inner dialogue became calmer and more constructive. Negative self-talk softened. Anxiety reduced.

Reading became emotional hygiene.

There were some days when reading was effortless and some days when it was like a struggle. I did not resist either. I trusted the rhythm.

Some days, a few pages were sufficient.
Some days, a chapter just flowed with itself.
Consistency was more important than quantity.
Reading daily also created a sense of continuity from day to day. It provided me with something to come back to, a quiet place that waited patiently.

This continuity was grounding.
Reading also taught me to have discernment.
I became more selective about what I had in my mind. Not everything was worthy of attention. Not all opinions required engagement. Reading made values clear and values directed choice.

This discernment gave me less mental overload.
Over time, reading no longer felt like a habit, but it began to feel like nourishment. I missed it when I skipped it, not due to guilt, but due to awareness.

That awareness was an indicator of integration.
This chapter is important because the quality of how we think influences the quality of the way we live. Reading is one of the

surest means of raising just that quality, quietly, consistently, deeply.

Reading does not shout.
It whispers.
But whispers, repeated daily, reshape inner landscapes.
Through reading, I learned that growth does not require constant striving. It requires steady exposure to ideas that stretch, soothe, and strengthen the mind.

Reading fed my mind the way walking fed my body and breathing fed my nervous system.
Together, these practices created balance.

With reading in place, the foundation was complete. The next phase of the journey is not about adding more habits, but about seeing the results of these quiet practices.
That is where we go next, into the shifts in health, mind, and performance that emerged naturally.

12

The Shift in My Health

The shift that I experienced in my health, that did not happen overnight.
I cannot say that there was a morning, I woke up, and I felt like I had changed, transformed.

Instead, the change came about in stealth. So stealthily that I could only recognize the change in retrospect.
Health, I learned, makes no announcement of its return.

It makes itself known softly, by the lack of struggle.

For a long time, I had treated health as something that was separate from daily living. It was something to be concerned with when things went wrong, not something to cultivate daily. As long as I could function, I assumed everything was fine.
I did not feel ill.

But I was not completely feeling well either.
There was a constant feeling of fatigue that I accepted as the norm. Energy fluctuated unpredictably. Some days were productive, others heavy. I ignored fatigue and pushed through it.
That pushing took a toll, one that I wasn't aware of until it started to disappear.

As I brought prayer, gratitude, breathing, walking, journaling, daily goals, and reading into my life, I did not do it as a means of improving my health as the main objective. I was looking for clarity, peace and alignment.
Health got better as a byproduct.

The first thing that I noticed was the energy stability.
Before, my energy level went up and down drastically. Mornings often felt rushed. Afternoons felt draining. Evenings left me depleted. I blamed workload, age or circumstances.
With the passage of time, energy became steadier.

I woke up feeling more rested. And that was not necessarily because I got more sleep. It was like my body was calmer. My nervous system was no longer on constant-alert. Breathing and prayer made the shift from resting to doing gentler.

Energy ceased to be borrowed.

It felt owned.

Walking was a large part of this shift. Regular movement helped to restore circulation, release the stiffness and bring rhythm to my body. I was no longer sedentary for extended periods of time. My body felt used rather than ignored.

Walking did not exhaust me.

It energized me.

Another significant shift was toward better-quality sleep.

Before these practices, sleep was irregular. Some nights were restful, others restless. My mind was often active long after I went to bed. Thoughts re-lived the day, or projected tomorrow.

As my days became more structured and reflective, my nights became more calm. Journaling helped to clear the mental residue. Gratitude alleviated emotional tension. Breathing slowed down the nervous system.

Sleep deepened naturally.

I stopped chasing sleep.

I allowed it.

This improvement in itself had a cascading effect on health. Better sleep equaled better focus, better mood, better resilience.

The body reacts rapidly when consistent messages of safety and rhythm are given.

Another noticeable change was a decrease in physical tension. Earlier in my life my body held tension that I was not aware of. Shoulders rigid. Jaws tight. Shallow breaths. Stress had become muscular.

Through breathing and walking consciously, that tension began to release. I noticed that I improved my posture. My breathing deepened. My movements become more fluid.

This release was not dramatic.

It was cumulative.

The body was let go of because it no longer had to stay guarded.

Health also improved with the increased body awareness.

Before, I ignored little signals. Fatigue meant working harder. Discomfort equaled distraction. Hunger, rest and movement signals were overridden.

Through these practices, I learned to listen.

It made me intelligent.

I adjusted effort on the basis of energy. I rested without guilt. I moved without forcing. This responsiveness helped avoid burnout.

Health became no longer reactive.

It became proactive.

Another shift took place in my relationship to stress.

Stress did not disappear. Life remained demanding. Responsibilities continued. But my ability to cope with stress improved.

Breathing created a pause.

Walking created release.

Journaling brought about understanding.

Stress no longer accumulated.

Instead of carrying it around silently, I processed it every day.

This prevented stress from becoming exhaustion.

One of the deepest changes was the lightness in my body.

Not lightness like in weight, but lightness like in ease. Movements felt less heavy. Tasks felt less taxing. Even busy days were bearable.

This ease was provided by alignment.

When mind, breath, and body are working in conjunction, there is less effort.

Health also improved emotionally.

In the past, emotional ups and downs had an impact on my physical condition. Irritation drained energy. Anxiety tightened the body. Restlessness interfered with sleep.

As emotional regulation improved with gratitude, journaling, and breathing, physical well-being followed.

The body makes no distinction between emotional and physical stress.

It responds to both.

By working on the inner states, I worked on health in a holistic manner.

Another important shift was consistency.

Health is often pursued in bursts, periods of enthusiasm and then neglect. My approach changed. Instead of excessive labor, I preferred gentle caretaking.

Walking daily.

Breathing consciously.

Resting intentionally.

These little acts built resilience.

I also stopped thinking of health as a goal to be reached. I began thinking of it as a relationship to be nurtured.

A relationship requires attention, respect, and patience.

This view eliminated pressure.

Health was not another item on my to do list.

It was like a companion to be taken care of.

Over time, my immune response improved. Minor discomforts went away quicker. Recovery became smoother. I did not analyze these changes too much. I just got a general impression of robustness.

The body felt supported.

Another subtle change was a change in confidence in my physical self.

Former uncertainty in energy and stamina caused hesitation. My concern was overexertion or burnout. As my own health stabilized, there was more confidence.

I trusted my body.

Trust reduces fear.

Fear drains energy.

This trust carried over into work and everyday life. I got more

involved, knowing that I could recover and recalibrate.
Health also had an effect on my mood baseline.
Earlier, mood was subject to fluctuation depending on the circumstances. One thing with improved health is the mood stabilized. I felt calmer, more patient, more even keeled.
This stability led to better relations and decision making.

Health is not merely physical capacity.
It is emotional steadiness.
I also saw how health affected my sense of dignity.
Caring for my body was a matter of respecting myself. I was no longer using my body to perform. I was honoring it as a partner.
This respect led to a deeper understanding of discipline that was natural.

When you respect something, you take care of it and don't resent it.
There were days when I fell short. Days when routines broke. Days when energy dipped. I did not treat those days as failures.
Health is not linear.
It is adaptive.

Returning gently mattered more than staying perfect.
This compassionate approach ensured continuity.
This chapter matters because many people seek health through external interventions while ignoring daily rhythms. True health

emerges when daily life supports the body rather than drains it.
My health improved. Not because I chased it aggressively. But because I stopped undermining it unconsciously.

Prayer reduced inner noise.
Gratitude softened emotional strain.
Breathing regulates stress.
Walking restored movement.
Journaling cleared the mind.
Daily goals reduced chaos.
Reading enriched perspective.
Health was the natural outcome.

The shift in my health taught me an important lesson. The body responds quickly when it feels safe, heard, and respected.
Health is not something you force.
It is something you allow.

This realization prepared me for the next shift, one that occurred quietly alongside physical health: the shift in my mind. That is where we go next.

13

The Calm That Replaced Chaos

People think of calm as silence. But to me, it did not come like that.
It arrived as space.

For a long time, my inner world was full. Thoughts overlapped. Concerns contended for attention. Emotions remained for longer than necessary. Even on days when I felt like everything was going to be okay externally, inside my head, I was busy.
I had accepted this as normal.

In its place, I thought mental noise was merely the price you pay.

Price for responsibility, ambition, and modern life. I assumed that calm was something that happened from time to time. During holidays. In moments of escape. After something was finally taken care of.

What I did not understand at the time was this.

Calm is not the absence of doing anything. It is the presence of order.

As the practices slowly took root in my life, prayer, gratitude, breathing, walking, journaling, daily goals, and reading, I was not consciously seeking calm. I was just trying to live in a more aware and consistent way.

Calm came without much noise or fanfare.

The first shift I saw was a decrease in mental clutter.

Earlier, my mind had too many unfinished loops. Pending tasks, conversations left unsaid, decisions postponed, thoughts left unsaid, everything was still in the background. Even when I was resting physically, my mind was not at rest.

Journaling and daily reflection started closing these loops.

Writing things down allowed my mind to let go. What had seemed overwhelming became manageable. Thoughts ceased to be circulating endlessly and came to a standstill.

This alone brought relief.

Another notable change was slowed thinking.

Not dull thinking.

Not indecision.

But deliberate thinking.

Earlier, my mind went from one conclusion to another with great rapidity. I reacted before fully understanding situations. I spoke before I heard all the way through. My thinking was quick, but not necessarily always clear.

With regular breathing and reflection, my thinking slowed just enough to gain depth.

I paused before responding.

I listened more fully.

I thought about context before implementing the action.

That pause altered everything.

Calm has been brought into my life through these little pauses, between stimulus and response, between thinking and doing, between effort and rest.

Those pauses created choice.

And choice created freedom.

Emotionally, the change was equally marked.

In the past, emotions swept me along. Irritation escalated. Anxiety lingered. Disappointment felt heavy. I felt emotions to the fullest, but without control.

Through gratitude and breath awareness and journaling, emotions, without domination, found expression. I could feel without being overwhelmed.

Not being emotionally upset does not mean being calm.
It means being emotionally capable.
This capacity shifted my relationship with difficult feelings. Instead of fighting the discomfort, I let it go through. Breathing was used to control intensity. Journaling allowed for the processing of meaning. Gratitude provided a balance in perspective.
Emotions no longer piled up.

Another important change was the reduction of anticipation stress. Earlier, I had so much of my mental muscle occupied with worrying about the future, of the things that had not happened yet, of conversations and possibilities. My mind was living in the future, away from the moment.

Daily intentions and prayer brought me back to the present moment.
When the day was clear, tomorrow was bearable. When mornings dawned in silence, doubt was softened.

I ceased to carry tomorrow into today unnecessarily.

Calm also manifested itself as clarity.

Decisions became simpler. Not because choices vanished, but because priorities became clear. I knew what mattered. I knew what could wait.

This clarity got rid of overthinking. Overthinking lives in ambiguity. Clarity dissolves it.

As my inner state was calmer, I found that I was listening to others better.

Earlier on, even in the middle of listening, my mind was getting my responses ready. I heard words but not always the meaning of the words. Calm allowed presence.

I listened without urgency.

I spoke with intention.

Conversations were less transactional and more authentic. Misunderstandings reduced. Relationships softened.

Calm also made a difference to my inner dialogue.

A few years ago, my inner voice was nagging and critical. It pushed all the time and seldom recognized effort. Through constant practice, that voice softened.

I became kinder to myself. Not indulgent, but understanding. I stopped treating myself like a problem to be solved and started treating myself like a person to be supported.

Inner kindness led to less inner friction.

And inner friction is exhausting.

Another subtle but powerful shift was that of trust.

Earlier, I attempted to control results with my mind. I re-played scenarios, over-prepared and worried about things that I had no control over. Calm came when I learnt to trust processes.

Surrender developed through prayer.

Gratitude developed acceptance.

Breathing discriminated presence.

Together, they alleviated the need to control everything.

Control loosened.

Trust strengthened.

This trust was not passive. I still planned, worked hard, and took responsibility. But on me, there was constant supervision in the mind.

Calm replaced vigilance.

I also saw how calm affected my sense of time.

Earlier, time felt scarce. I rushed even when I did not need to.

Calm expanded time, not in an objective way, but experientially. When the mind is calm, moments are more full. Activities are less compressed. Presence is a stretch of experience.

Time felt generous.

Calm also made being silent comfortable.

Earlier, silence felt uneasy. I packed it with noise, screens, thoughts, tasks. Calm enabled me to sit with myself without being uncomfortable.

Silence became nourishing.

This ease with silence deepened reflection and self-awareness.

Importantly, calm didn't cause me to be detached from life. It made me engaged, not agitated.

I cared deeply.

I worked sincerely.

I felt fully.

But without chaos.

This distinction matters.

Chaos is not intensity. Chaos is a lack of order.

Calm is not dullness. Calm is clarity.

There were days when calm was tenuous. Days when stress resurfaced. Days when old patterns were back.

I did not resist those days.

Calm is not a permanent state.

It is a condition that is supported by practice.

Returning to the practices brought back balance.

Breathing calmed the body.

Walking released tension.

Journaling cleared the mind.

Prayer put things back into perspective.

Calm became recoverable.

This recoverability was empowering.

Earlier, stress was a feeling of being consumed. Now, it felt temporary.

Calm also affected my ability to concentrate.

Distractions reduced. Attention stabilized. I could do tasks longer without mental fatigue.

Focus became natural.

This was not involuntary concentration.

It was easy assimilation.

Calm was also a factor in creativity.

Ideas occurred without straining. Connections developed organically. Solutions appeared quietly.

The mind is at its best when it is not pressured.
One of the most meaningful of the effects of calm was inner confidence.

Not confidence rooted in achievement. But confidence rooted in steadiness. I trusted my ability to meet situations calmly, even when outcomes were uncertain.

This confidence reduced fear.
Fear thrives in chaos.
Calm dissolves it.

This chapter matters because many people seek calm by escaping life, through withdrawal, distraction, or avoidance. My experience taught me that calm comes from organizing the inner world, not abandoning the outer one.
Calm is not found.
It is cultivated.

And it is cultivated through small, consistent practices that support the mind and body every day.

The calm that replaced chaos did not make my life perfect.
It made it grounded, manageable, and meaningful.

From this calm emerged another shift, one that surprised me deeply.

As my mind settled and my body stabilized, my performance improved, not through pressure, but through clarity.
That is where the journey continues.

14

Performance Without Burnout

For a long time, I thought that to perform, you had to be under pressure.

I figured the harder I pushed myself, the more I demanded, and the harder I worked, the better things would become. To my mind, effort was inextricably linked with strain. If I wasn't tired, I thought I wasn't doing enough.

This belief influenced the way I worked, the way I measured success, and the way I treated myself.

It also silently guided me towards burnout.

Burnout does not occur overnight.

It is built up slowly. Through constant urgency. Through unrelenting expectations. Through the lack of recovery.
Before the shift, my performance was very dependent on adrenaline. Deadlines energized me. Pressure sharpened focus. Crisis-triggered action. I was able to perform well, with some limitations on time.

In between these bursts of work, there was exhaustion.
This cycle was something that felt familiar and normal. Many of the people around me lived the same way. High effort followed by tiring. Intensity followed by exhaustion.

What I didn't realize back then was that this was not sustainable performance. It was a survival performance.
As the practices became part of my daily routine, prayer, gratitude, breathing, walking, journaling, daily goals, and reading, the relationship with work began to change.

Not immediately.
Not dramatically.
But fundamentally.

The first shift was understanding of effort.
Earlier on, I used to spend energy all over the place. Tasks blended together. Urgency determined priorities. I was busy, but not

necessarily effective. I confused activity with impact.
Daily goals changed this.

By determining what mattered and what did not day in and day out, effort got focused. I no longer managed to scatter my energy across too many tasks. I invested it deliberately.

Focused effort has a lighter quality to it than spread-out effort.
This focus was enough to improve performance.
The second shift was energy management.

In the past, I attempted to control time without controlling energy. I packed my schedule without thinking of capacity. Some tasks required deep focus, others required interaction, but I treated them all the same.

Through awareness and reflection, I started matching tasks to energy levels. I used to work on demanding things when my mind was fresh. I planned lighter work when energy was low.
This alignment decreased friction.

Work was easier, not because it was really easy, but because it was better timed.
Another significant change was less mental interference.
Earlier, my mind used to be against me. Worry, self-doubt,

overthinking, and unnecessary pressure were a drain on energy. Even when tasks were manageable, the mental noise made them feel heavy.

Calm served to reduce this interference.
Breathing regulates stress.
Prayer decreased the inner pressure.
Gratitude balanced perspective.

With fewer internal distractions, the performance just naturally improved.

The mind was no longer an opponent, but a friend.
I also noticed that the focus became deeper.
Earlier, attention became fragmented easily. Notifications, interruptions, and inner restlessness constantly took me away. Focus required effort.

As my inner state became more stable, it was easier to focus. I could remain with a task for a longer period of time without getting tired. I went into the flow more often.
Flow is not forced.

It comes into play when the resistance is less.
Calm provided conditions for flow.

Another significant change was the quality of the decision-making. Earlier, the decisions were rushed. Pressure called for rapid answers. I responded to situations rather than consider them.

With better clarity and composure, decisions slowed just enough to be wiser. I considered implications. I chose deliberately.
Better decisions resulted in a reduction in rework.

Reduced rework saved energy.
This resulted in a positive cycle.
Performance also improved because of learning to stop earlier.
Earlier, I used to work till exhaustion made me stop. I ignored signals of fatigue. Rest felt like weakness.

Through body awareness and respect for limits, I learned to stop before depletion. Short breaks replenished the energy supply. Walking reset focus. Breathing rebalanced the nervous system.
Rest became strategic, rather than accidental.
This prevented burnout.

Another subtly powerful shift was emotional neutrality at work. Emotions were a big factor in performance previously. Praise elevated me. Criticism unsettled me. Defeats killed motivation.

As emotional regulation got better, work was less personal. I kept

myself engaged without being emotionally caught up.
This neutrality enhanced resiliency.

I was able to accept feedback without being defensive.
I could deal with setbacks with no discouragement.
I could celebrate victories without being attached to them.
This balance made performance stable.
I also found better consistency.

Earlier, the performance varied. There were some days when it was incredibly productive, and others when it was a sluggish day. Motivation varied.
With daily practices, performance stabilized. Not peak every day, but steady. Predictable. Reliable.

Consistency is underrated.
Sustainable performance is not about peaks.
It is about being reliable over time.
Another significant change was congruence between effort and values.

Earlier, I worked hard, but not always in a meaningful way. Some effort was felt draining because it lacked alignment.
Through reflection and clarity, I was able to start making more conscious choices about what I was creating that had a deeper

meaning. Even when tasks were demanding, when alignment was present, resistance was lowered.

Aligned effort has a sense of purpose.

Purpose reduces fatigue.

Performance improved because effort was meaningful.

Reading also played an important role.

Exposure to ideas was a boost to the quality of thinking. I came to challenges with a greater perspective. I learned from other people's experiences, not making the avoidable mistakes.

This intellectual food improved the strategic thinking.

Better thinking results in better performance.

Another important change was the decreased urgency.

Urgency creates stress. Stress narrows thinking. Narrow thinking is not very effective.

As calm increased, the urgency decreased. I stopped treating everything as an emergency. I made a distinction between what was important and what was just loud.

This lowered pressure brought about an improvement in output quality.

I also learned to say no, without guilt.

Earlier, I overcommitted. I set myself for more than I could hold.

Saying no was uncomfortable.

Daily goals and clarity allowed me to maintain focus. I declined distractions. I chose depth over breadth.
This improved the results.

Performance also improved because I learned to measure differently.
Earlier, I measured performance in terms of output volume and visible effort. Long hours equaled success.

Now, the measurement of performance was based on clarity, impact, and sustainability. I preferred being effective to being exhausted.

This redefinition altered behaviour.
I stopped glorifying being busy.
I respected recovery.
I valued quality.

Burnout occurs when effort outpaces recovery on a regular basis.
My practices made sure recovery was part of everyday life.
Breathing restored calm.
Walking restored energy.

Prayer put things into perspective.
Journaling brought things back into perspective.

Burnout had no fertile ground.

There were days when work was strenuous. There were deadlines, challenges, and high-pressure situations. Performance was not effortless. But it became manageable.
Manageability is the antidote to burnout.
I trusted the fact that I could engage fully and be able to recover adequately.

This trust reduced anxiety.
Another profound shift was confidence without aggression.
Earlier, confidence came from pushing harder and proving capability. Now, confidence came from steadiness and preparation.

I trusted my systems.
I trusted my habits.
I trusted my capacity.

This quiet confidence improved leadership and collaboration.
Performance without burnout is not about doing less.
It is about doing what matters, with clarity, consistency, and care.

This chapter matters because burnout is often mistaken for a personal weakness rather than a systemic issue. Burnout occurs when effort is disconnected from recovery and meaning.

My experience taught me that high performance and well-being are not opposites. They are partners.

When the inner world is organized, the outer world becomes manageable.
Performance improved not because I tried harder, but because I lived better.
The practices did not slow me down.
They stabilized me.
From that stability, effectiveness emerged naturally.

This realization prepared me for a deeper insight, one that reframed everything I thought I knew about discipline.

15

Discipline Is an Act of Self-Love

For most of my life, I got discipline wrong.

I saw it as something austere. Inflexible routines. Strict rules. Unremitting self-control. In my mind, discipline meant forcing myself. To push myself to do the things I was not interested in. It felt like denial. It felt like I was restricting myself. It felt like I was sacrificing things.

At first, I resisted it. That was natural.

I admired the people who were disciplined. But only from afar. I didn't want to be one of them. Discipline felt heavy. It felt joyless. It was as if it were a constant struggle with oneself.

What I didn't know at the time was that the discipline I was rejecting was not the discipline of transformation. It was the discipline of punishment.

My journey taught me, in a slow way, a different truth: True discipline is self-love.

This realization did not come from theory. It emerged from experience.

As I practiced prayer, gratitude, breathing, walking, journaling, daily goals, and reading, the practice of discipline entered my life silently. Not as force but consistency. Not as control but as commitment.

And it was nothing like what I had feared.

Discipline, as I experienced it, was mild.

It was the act of showing up for myself, especially on ordinary days. It was making a choice to care for my inner world before reacting to the outer world. It was forming a structure not to limit myself, but to support myself.

This type of discipline had a nurturing effect.

For the first time, discipline was not energy draining.

It restored it.

I started to understand discipline as a sign of respect. When you have respect for something, you take care of it. You don't abuse it. You don't neglect it. You don't exploit it for your short-term gain.

I had spent years respecting deadlines, commitments, and expectations, but not necessarily myself.

Discipline had corrected that imbalance.

Prayer was a discipline.

Gratitude was a discipline.

Breathing was a discipline.

Walking was a discipline.

Journaling was a discipline.

Yet all of these felt nothing like punishment.

They felt grounded.

This is when I understood that discipline is not to say "no" to life.

It is about saying "yes" to the things that are important.

The lack of discipline is often passed off as freedom. In reality, the lack of discipline is the cause of chaos - mental, emotional, and physical. Chaos drains energy. Chaos creates anxiety. Chaos fragments attention.

Discipline is the means of freedom by producing order.

When my days remained unstructured, my mind did too. When my habits were all over the place, my energy was too. When my inner world was neglected, my outer performance was affected.

Discipline brought order.
Order brought calm.
Calm brought clarity.
Clarity brought with it effectiveness.
This chain was undeniable.

Another very important thing that I realised was this. Discipline never asks you for perfection.
Earlier, missing a single day felt like failure. That belief caused discipline to be fragile. One habit missed would spiral out into abandonment.

Self-loving discipline doesn't crumble when imperfect.
If I missed a prayer, I came back the next day and did it.
If I didn't take a walk today, I would return to it tomorrow.
If writing in a journal was difficult for me, I wrote less, not nothing.

Going back was more important than keeping streaks.
Self-love does not penalize inconsistency.
It encourages return.
This approach contributed to resilience.

Discipline also taught me to be patient.
Growth is slow. Integration takes time. Habits do not change life overnight. Discipline requires you to have faith in the process, especially when one doesn't see results right away.

This patience allowed for less frustration.
Instead of asking, "Why isn't this working yet?"
I started to ask, "Am I showing up today?"
That changed everything.

Discipline also altered my self-speaking.
Earlier, my inner discourse was demanding and critical. "You should be doing more." "You are falling behind." "You're not quite disciplined enough.

That voice, through a lot of consistent practice, grew soft.
It began to sound like this:
“Take care.”
“Return gently.”
“Stay consistent.”

Discipline was supportive instead of aggressive.
This support strengthened commitment.
Another insight was that discipline thrives on clarity. Motivation has little to do with it.

Motivation fluctuates. Discipline does not disappear if it is grounded in values.

Discipline was not achieved by inspiration every day, but by understanding the reason behind these practices. They supported my health. They stabilized my mind. They increased my performance.

That understanding gave rise to devotion.

Devotion is a discipline that has meaning.

Discipline also helped me to set boundaries.

Self-love needs boundaries. Without them, energy seeps out everywhere. I learnt to protect mornings. I learned to protect rest. I learned to protect focus.

Saying no was easier when I knew what I was saying yes to.

Discipline taught me that boundaries are not walls.

They are containers.

Containers enable life to flow with meaning.

Another profound realization was that discipline is incredibly compassionate.

It accepts humans and their limitations. It accepts the fact that energy is changing. It provides for flexibility without abandoning.

Self-loving discipline changes.

On low-energy days, discipline meant to do less, not nothing. On busy days, discipline was about simplification. On hard days, the discipline involved getting back to basics, breath, prayer, and presence.

This flexibility ensured that the discipline would be sustainable.
Discipline also changed my relationship with time.
Time previously felt like something chasing me. Through discipline, time became something I stewarded. Each day seemed planned rather than just a chance happening.

This stewardship helped to reduce anxiety.
I gave up trying to get the most out of each hour. I was concentrating on meaningful engagement.
Discipline brought dignity to time.
Another change was the way I was disciplined and how it impacted my identity.

Earlier, I thought of myself as someone who had a hard time being consistent. Through repeated practice, that identity silently changed.

I became someone who returns.
Someone who practices.
Someone who cares.

Identity follows behavior.

Discipline made me who I was becoming; no big declarations.

Discipline also increased humility.

I gave up on trying to master life. I learned to tend to it. Discipline is not about domination. It is about cultivation.

You don't force growth.

You create conditions for it.

This attitude helped to take the pressure off and foster a sense of trust.

Spiritually, discipline brought me into alignment with something deeper.

Daily acts became acts of remembrance, remembrance of values, purpose, and presence. Discipline allowed me to be in touch with meaning even when life was demanding.

It prevented drift.

This chapter is important because there are many people who reject discipline because of a misunderstanding. They link it with rigidity, harshness, and deprivation. My experience would show me the opposite.

Discipline, when rooted in self-love, is liberating.

It creates safety within routine.

It creates calm within structure.

It creates freedom within form.

Discipline does not shrink life.

It supports it.

Looking back, I realize that every meaningful shift in my life required discipline. But none of it ever demanded cruelty. It asked for consistency. But it never demanded punishment. It asked for commitment. But it never thought about self-betrayal.

This understanding changed how I approached everything.

Discipline became a daily act of saying:

"I matter enough to show up."

"My well-being matters."

"My inner life deserves care."

That is self-love in action.

And from that place of self-love emerged a final, powerful realization. One that ties everything together.

Perfection was never required.

Only practice was.

That insight forms the foundation of the next chapter.

16

You Don't Need a Perfect Day, Just a Practiced One

For a very long time, I used to believe that perfect days mattered to make progress in life.

I thought that everything had to go right if habits were to work. I needed time, I needed energy, I needed the right mood, and I needed focus, and I needed to have it uninterrupted. If any of these were missing, I assumed that the day was compromised.
And once a day was felt to be compromised, I treated it as lost.
This thinking sabotaged the consistency in silence.

I would start off with enthusiasm, follow a routine for a while, miss a day or two, become disappointed, and give up altogether. Perfection became the norm, and perfection, as usual, was beyond reach.

What I did not know then was a simple truth: Transformation does not need to take place on perfect days. It requires practice.
This realization changed the way I approached everything.
A day of practice is not an ideal day.
It is a return day.
It is a day you return to what is important - imperfectly, briefly, sincerely.

When I gave up demanding perfect days, discipline was humane.
In the past, failure to keep a habit was a sense of failure. Now, it felt like information. Instead of asking, "Why did I fail?" I started asking, "How can I go back today?"
That question took the edge off resistance.

Life is unpredictable. Some days are heavy. Some days are crowded. There are days that are emotionally draining. Expecting perfection in this reality is unrealistic and unkind.
The reality is accepting practice day. It works with it.
On a practiced day, prayer may be two minutes instead of twenty. Gratitude may be a single line of honesty instead of a list.

Breathing may be one extended pause. Walking might be shorter. Journaling might be sparse.
All of it still counts.

Because practice is not about intensity, it's about continuity.
This shift removed guilt.
Guilt drains energy.
Gentle return restores it.

What I learned was that missing a practice is not a problem. The problem is abandoning the practice due to that miss.
A practiced day is a day that you don't allow one imperfection to define the entire day.

This philosophy provided tremendous relief.
Earlier, I was burdened with "shoulds."
I should have done more.
I should have done better.
I should have been constant.

And those 'shoulds' put pressure on. Pressure led to avoidance.
Practiced days replaced pressure by permission.
Permission to show up as I was.
Permission to adjust.
Permission to return.

This permission allowed for the sustainability of the discipline. Another important realization was that practiced days are cumulative and silent.

One day of practice may not seem revolutionary. Ten may not either. But over a period of weeks and months, their effect is undeniable.

Practiced days compound.
They shape identity.
They shape perception.
They shape behavior.
Perfection requires results.
Practice builds foundations.

I further learned that practiced days involve being honest.
Some days, the most honest thing to do is rest. Some days, it is being silent. Some days, it is just acknowledging, "Today is hard."
Practice and action are not necessarily the same.

Sometimes, it means acceptance.
This acceptance was what prevented burnout.
I stopped pushing on those days I shouldn't have pushed. I gave up the pressure to be productive when presence was required. I learned to listen.

Listening is a practice, too.

Practiced days also helped to improve resiliency.

In the past, my life was thrown off course by disruptions. A skipped routine would get out of hand into disengagement. With this mindset, there were disruptions that became part of the rhythm.

I expected interruptions.

I planned for imperfection.

I trusted the return.

This trust stabilised things.

Practiced days also changed my relationship with motivation.

I stopped waiting to feel ready.

Readiness is unreliable.

Return is dependable.

I practiced even when I did not feel like it, gently, briefly, imperfectly. And often, practice made the preparation rather than the other way around.

This overturned the old pattern.

Another powerful shift was the reduction of self-judgment as a result of practiced days.

Earlier, I was extremely hard on myself. I compared my efforts to unreasonable standards. I wrote progress off because it wasn't impressive.

Practiced days taught me to measure differently.
Did I return today?
Did I show up honestly?
Did I care, even briefly?
Those became the metrics.
These metrics gave confidence.

Confidence based on practice is quiet, steady, and resilient.
Practiced days also led to better emotional regulation.
On hard days, instead of spiraling into frustration, I went back to basics: breath, gratitude, walking. I did not demand productivity. I demanded presence.

Presence made the difficulty easier.
This approach helped to change the way I navigated stress.
I stopped trying to “fix” days.
I started meeting them.
Meeting the day as it is, without resistance, resulted in less inner conflict.
Inner conflict is tiring.
Acceptance is energy-conserving.
Another insight was that momentum is protected by practiced days.

Momentum is fragile when founded on perfection. It is robust if it is built on return.

Even in cases where practices felt minimal, the momentum was still retained. There was no need to restart. I was already on the path.

This continuity was of the utmost importance.
Days of humility were also practiced.
I gave up trying to be disciplined, to myself or to others. I accepted my humanity. I accepted fluctuations.

This humbleness ensured that this growth became honest.
Growth does not require heroic effort.
It requires faithful return.
Spiritually, the days taught me devotion over drama.
Devotion shows up quietly.
Drama demands attention.

Prayer imperfectly done is better than prayer perfectly done too late. Gratitude feebly felt is better than gratitude not felt at all. Breath briefly noticed is better than breath ignored.
Consistency is better than intensity.
It was through this understanding that there was peace.
Peace is not found in the control of life.

It originates from cooperating with it.

Practiced days also led to a shift in my thinking over the long haul. I quit worrying about what was going to happen. I focused on today's return. One practiced day at a time.
This simplified everything.
Life became manageable.

Not because it got easier, but because I stopped expecting impossible standards.
Practiced days also brought a sense of trust in myself.
Each return reinforced the belief: I can come back.

I don't disappear when I am struggling.
I don't abandon myself when things get messy.
This trust was healing.
Many people fail not due to lack of discipline, but lack of self-forgiveness.

Practiced days help one develop forgiveness through action.
You forgive by returning.
You heal by continuing.
This chapter is relevant because perfectionism is a silent killer of progress. It hides behind the guise of high standards, but what it does is convert consistency into impossibility.

Practice liberates the effort of fear.

When the fear of failure is gone, action is lighter.
By embracing practice days, I learned that life does not require flawless execution. It requires honest participation.

Some days are strong.
Some days are quiet.
Some days are messy.
All of them can be practiced.

This philosophy allowed everything else in my life to stabilize. Habits stayed alive. Calm remained accessible. Performance stayed sustainable.

Most importantly, I stopped being at war with myself.
A practiced day is a peaceful day, even when it is imperfect.
And from this peace emerged the final invitation of this journey.
Not to copy my practices.
Not to follow a rigid system.
But to begin, where you are.
That is where the book now turns outward, to you, the reader.

17

Start From Where You Are

There is a quiet temptation that follows every story of transformation.

It is the temptation to compare.

As you read about changes/practices/progress, a little voice may emerge:

I'm not there yet.

I don't have that discipline.

My life is more complicated.

That voice is natural.

And it is precisely why this chapter is important.

Because the most important truth of all I have learned in this journey is this: You do not need to start where I am.

You just have to start where you're at.

Transformation does not start with ambition.

It begins with honesty.

Honesty about energy.

Honesty about capacity.

Honesty in life as it is.

For a long time, I held out on changing because I felt like I had to have better conditions to change. More time. Less responsibility. More clarity. Fewer distractions.

Those conditions never came.

Life does not stop to make a place for transformation. Transformation occurs within the confines of life.

Starting where you are involves accepting reality but not fighting it.

It means saying:

This is my life today.

This is my energy today.

This is my capacity today.

And then posing a simple question: What is one small act of care I can give myself today?

That question is powerful.
It moves from outcome to activity.
From ideal to available.
From perfection to presence.

Many people never start because they wait until they feel ready.
Readiness is a myth.
You do not become ready and then start.
You start out, and then there is readiness.

I did not begin my journey as one who was disciplined. I started feeling scattered. I did not start off with confidence. I began with curiosity. I did not start with structure. I began with a pause.
That pause was enough.

Starting where you are does not mean that you have to accept stagnation.
It means accepting where you are starting from.
Acceptance is not resignation.
It is clarity.
Clarity allows movement.

One of the very liberating things for me was this: weak beginnings don't mean you began small.
They are sustainable beginnings.

A few minutes of prayer is sufficient.
A short walk is enough.
It only requires a single line of gratitude.
A little time to breathe is sufficient.
Enough to begin.

When you are starting where you are, you are removing the burden of performance. You stop trying to impress yourself. You cease measuring effort against some imagined standard.
You show up honestly.

Honest effort is faster than heroic effort.
Another key part to starting where you are is to let go of timelines. Transformation does not work on schedules. It unfolds at its own pace. When you rush it, you interfere with it. When you allow it, it deepens.

There is no time limit for becoming disciplined.
There is no age limit for clarity.
There is no ideal season for starting.
Now is enough.

Starting where you are also means working with the resistance rather than fighting it.
Resistance is not the enemy.
It is information.

When something feels hard, it tells you something about energy, fear, or overload. Instead of being forced through resistance, soften the practice.

If journaling seems like a lot, write less.
If you find walking tiring, do it more slowly.
If praying feels far away, sit in silence.
Meet resistance with curiosity, not judgment.
This approach keeps practices alive.

Another gentle truth: You do not need all the practices at one time. I did not adopt things all at once. Each practice entered my life at the time I was ready to receive it. They grew organically rather than strategically.
You can start with one practice.

Or half of one.
Or the idea of one.
That is enough.
Transformation is not a matter of adding more.

It is about integration slowly.

Starting where you are is also a way to honor your life circumstances.

Your responsibilities are important. Your constraints are real. Your challenges are valid. Discipline does not entail withdrawal from life. It calls for engagement with it, self-consciously.

Do not wait to make life easier.

Allow practices to make life steadier.

Another important shift that comes from starting where you are is trust.

Trust in the process.

Trust in return.

Trust in yourself.

Trust is increased when you keep small promises. When you show up gently. When you go back without a fuss.

Intensity does not create trust.

It comes from reliability.

And reliability is developed one practice day at a time.

Starting where you are also means accepting fluctuation.

Some days you will feel committed. Some days you won't. Some days, practices will feel nourishing. Some days they will feel mechanical.

Do not overinterpret this.

Consistency does not entail emotional consistency.

It requires presence.

Presence says: I am here today.

That is enough.

You might be wondering whether these little practices can really make a difference in your life. That doubt is natural.

Small things don't mean much until they add up.

One drop of water appears to be powerless.

But steady drops shape stone.

Your everyday choices impact your inner world in the same way.

Starting where you are and accumulating.

Another subtle gift of beginning where you are is that of being compassionate towards others.

As you show gentleness with yourself, you show gentleness with people around you. You quit demanding perfection. You allow humanity.

This softens relationships.

Transformation is not an individual achievement.

It changes the way you present yourself in the world.
Starting where you are also means no more comparing.
Your path will not be like mine.
It should not.

Your practices will be different in different shapes.
They should.
Your rhythm will be your own.

Comparison takes the attention away from the presence. Presence is where the growth occurs.

If there is one thing that I hope you take away from this chapter, it is this: You do not have to be someone else in order to live consciously.

Every single one of you needs to get more present as who you already are.

Start where you are with honesty, patience, and care.
Start with what you can stick to, not what looks good.
Just one small act of alignment today.
Tomorrow will take care of itself.

Transformation is not a destination that you arrive at.

It is a relationship you establish with yourself.

And relationships are built up by attention, not urgency.

So begin gently.

Begin honestly.

Begin now.

18

A Simple Daily Framework

This chapter is not an instruction manual.

It is an invitation.

After everything you have read, the drift, the pause, the practices, the shifts, it may be tempting to ask this.

So what exactly should I be doing every day?

That is a reasonable question. But it carries a quiet risk.

When we search for a flawless framework, we are apt to make a living execution. We substitute awareness with rules, presence with pressure. The very practices that are supposed to calm you down start to seem heavy.

That is not the point here.
What follows is not a system to follow rigidly.
It is a rhythm you can adapt.
Think of it as a container, rather than a cage.

A simple framework to follow every day is not about controlling your life. It is there to support it, especially on the days when it seems distant and energy is off.

This framework has come about naturally from my own journey. It was not designed all in advance. It developed gradually, through practice, return, and improvement.
You may shape it differently.
You should.

The Spirit of the Framework

Before we speak of mornings or evenings, it is important to know the spirit of this framework.

This is not about doing everything, every day.

It is about remembering what is important every day.

Some days will be full.

Some days will be quiet.

There will be some scattered days.

This framework is intended to address all of them.

Its purpose is simple:

To begin the day grounded

To pass the day consciously

To end the day in reflection

Nothing more.

The Morning: Begin Gently

How you start the day affects how you face the day.

At earlier stages of my life, mornings were sharp. I went from sleep to stimulation with no transition. The mind had entered noise before it had found clarity.

The morning framework that I follow now is a deliberately gentle one.

1. Stillness - Before Stimulation. Before the phone. Before the world. Before information.

Even a few minutes of stillness alters the tone of the day.

This may look like prayer.

Or silence.

Or simply sitting quietly.

The intention is not to accomplish anything.

It is to arrive.

To let the body wake up fully.

To allow the mind to settle for engaging.

Some mornings are longer. Some are brief. Both are valid.

2. A Moment of Gratitude

Not a long list.

Not forced positivity.

Just an acknowledgement or two.

Gratitude does not require enthusiasm.

It needs sincerity.

This is a time for the mind to gently shift from being wantful to being sufficient.

3. Conscious Breathing

A few slow breaths.

Nothing technical.

Breathing grounds awareness in the body. It helps remind the nervous system that it is safe to start the day without the pressure.

This moment is often less than a minute.

Its impact lasts much longer.

The Day: Move with Intention

The point of the day is not to accomplish everything.

It is to do what matters in the present moment.

1. One to Three Intention Set for the Day

I keep my daily goals few on purpose.

Not tasks.

Intentions.

They may be professional.

They may be personal.

They may be either emotional or relational.

The question I ask is simple: What would make this day feel aligned by evening?

Writing this down matters.

It clarifies attention.

These intentions are like a compass, not a whip.

2. Movement as Rhythm

Movement does not need a slot.

It needs permission.

Walking, stretching, or gentle movement throughout the day brings about a restorative balance. It clears the mind of residue and reconnects the body and mind.

Movement is not something that you earn after productivity.

It is what enables it.

3. Breathing Through Transitions

Transitions are powerful.

Before meetings.

After some difficult conversations.

Between tasks.

A single conscious breath taken during transitions can prevent emotional carryover. It resets attention.

This is one of the most useful disciplines that I've learned.The Evening: Close with Care

How you end the day is just as important as how you start it.

Earlier, my days were ended abruptly. I took unspoken thoughts to rest. Sleep became shallow.

Now, evenings are softer.

1. Reflection in the Form of Journaling

This does not need to be elaborate.

A few questions are enough:

What went well today?

What felt heavy?

What did I learn?

This reflection is not for judgment.

It is for understanding.

Journaling is the closure of mental loops. It allows the mind permission to rest.

2. Review Without Criticism

Review is not evaluation.

It is awareness.

If intentions were accomplished, acknowledge that fact.

If they weren't, notice why.

No self-criticism.

Only curiosity.

This helps keep learning alive, without the pressure.

3. Reading to Nourish the Mind

Reading before sleep changes the mind from stimulation to reflection. It prepares the nervous system to rest.

Even a few pages are enough.

The Most Important Rule: Adaptation

Some days will disrupt the framework.
Life will intervene.
Energy will dip.

Unforeseen demands will be made.
Do not abandon the framework because of this.
Adapt it.

On difficult days, stillness may be one breath. Gratitude may be a silent acknowledgment. Movement may be minimal. Journaling may be one line.

That still counts.
Return is more important than completion.

What This Framework Is Not

It is not a productivity system.

It is not a checklist for self-improvement.

It is not a measure of worth.

It is a support structure.

If at any time it becomes heavy for you, simplify it.

If it feels rigid, soften it.

If it feels forced, pause.

Discipline through kindness survives.

Why This Works

This framework is effective because it honors:

Human variability

Energy cycles

Emotional reality

It develops rhythm without being rigid.

It makes spirituality a part of daily life, not as a belief, but as an awareness.

Most importantly, it keeps you connected to yourself.

A Final Word to You

You don't need to live your life this way.

You need to live consciously, as it suits you for your life.

Let practices serve you.

Let discipline support you.

Let clarity guide you.

And when you drift, and you will, drift gently back.

That is the real framework.

One practice day at a time is sufficient.